Dahnmon's Fantastic Dream

Extra: Dahnmon's Poems

BY:

Colonel Charles Dahnmon Whitt

Published By:

Dahnmon Whitt Family Publishing
Post Office Box 831
Flatwoods, KY 41139
Phone 606-836-7997
http:dahnmonwhittfamily.com

Published: July 31.2012
ISBN 978-1-62407-037-0

Edited by Sharon Whitt and Larry Whitt

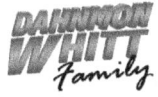

Dahnmon's Fantastic Dream
Contents

Colonel Charles Dahnmon Whitt

Dahnmon's Fantastic Dream

Preface

This is a tall tale or is it? Can a man journey back in time with his sub-conscience?

You will see a true account about the nature of our Native Americans. I tell the tale in fiction but use facts as to how they relate to the tale.

There is a Town Hill where once an Indian village stood. There is a County named Tazewell in Virginia, where a great river starts.

Go back with the Colonel as he tells this tale of back to the Indians in a fantastic dream.

Colonel Charles Dahnmon Whitt

Dahnmon's Fantastic Dream

My Transcending

I live in the twenty-first century with all the marvels of electronics and speeding automobiles.

I live a modern life with the exception that I love to read and do research on the past. I have often wondered what it would be like to go back in time and see our country in its virgin state. I always wanted to see how our Native Americans lived and how it all fit together. I wonder what they thought when they saw the first paleface in their world.

I had been having trouble sleeping so I had my doctor prescribe me some sleeping pills. After a busy day I had supper, watched a little television. I took my new sleeping pills and headed off to bed. After tossing and turning for about a minute I was out like a light.

An incredible thing happened next; I was transcended back in time to the deep woods of western Virginia to around 1600.

I looked around at all the great beauty of the land and vegetation about me. The whole area was covered with a great canopy of trees. I could hardly fathom the site as I gazed upon this great beauty.

Colonel Charles Dahnmon Whitt

Dahnmon's Fantastic Dream

The sun's rays crisscrossed through the high branches to create lumens' of heavenly light. I noticed the size of the tree trunks and guessed that most had to be 30 to 40 feet in circumference. I noticed that the woods floor was mostly clear of brush and that numerous trails crossed the vast woodland.

I heard many sounds as the birds and animals communicated with each other.

I looked at myself and even pinched my arm to see if it was me standing there taking it all in. Ouch! It was me, but how I got here I cannot imagine.

I looked at my wrist watch to see the time. According to my watch it was 3:05, but what day, month and year I had no idea. I had on my denim shorts, sport shoes and short ankle socks. I had on an old blue "T" shirt with the words, "Richlands High School." on it. This was the high school I attended back in the 1960's.

Colonel Charles Dahnmon Whitt

Dahnmon's Fantastic Dream

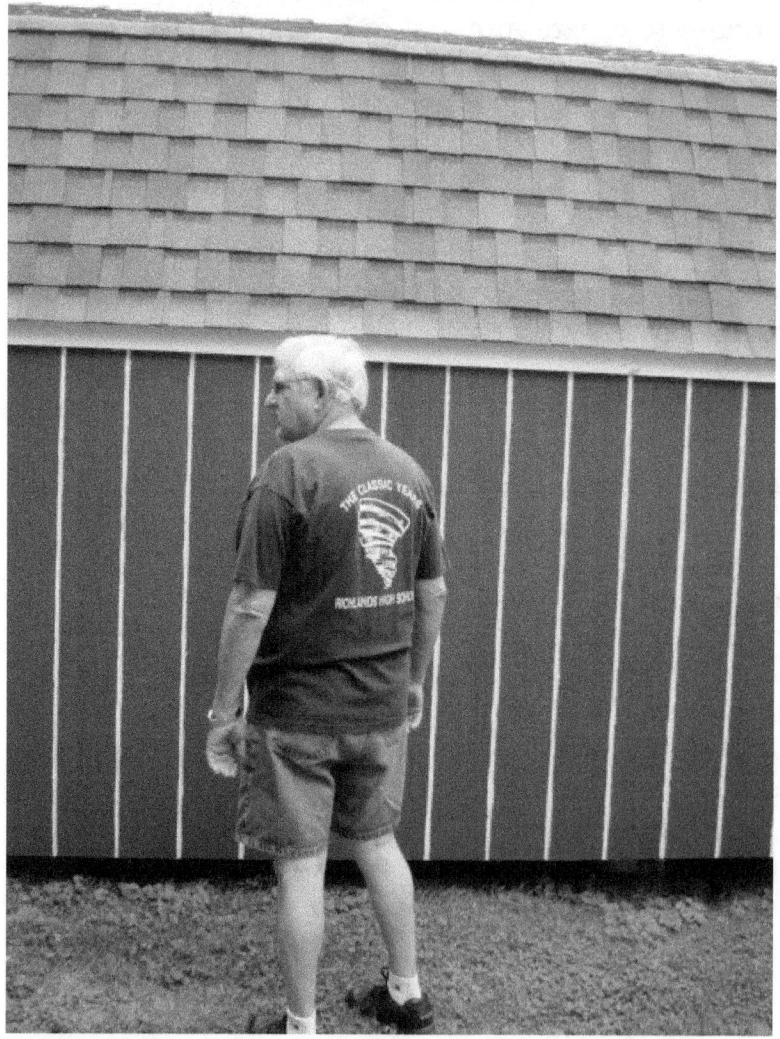

This is how I looked to the Indians

Colonel Charles Dahnmon Whitt

Dahnmon's Fantastic Dream

I had on my glasses which had the feature of darkening in bright light. In my left rear pocket I felt my wallet and checked it out. I had my 2012 Kentucky driver's license, some credit cards and a few dollars. In my front pocket I had a few coins and a small Case jack knife.

I wondered how I got to this beautiful place and how I would get back, if ever.

I was standing on a little bluff with a bigger mountain directly behind me. Looking down from the bluff I could see a stream of sparking water as the rays of light danced on its moving surface.

As I looked closer, motion caught my eye. My goodness, I saw a herd of elk grazing on a little pasture of green grass. I had never in my life looked upon such a sight. There must have been thirty or more of the majestic animals in the herd.

Lord, am I in heaven or have I lost my mind, I wondered.

I looked closer at my surroundings and I could see countless trails meandering through the forest floor. There must be an abundance of game to leave so many trails.

I wondered if there may be things about me that I should fear, but had no fear at the time. I looked

Colonel Charles Dahnmon Whitt

Dahnmon's Fantastic Dream

about another time and calculated that I must be living in the past some four-hundred years. I felt like I knew this place somehow, or had been there before.

I could see great ferns and some of the ground was covered with a sea of deep green moss the likes of which I had never seen before. I reasoned that I must be on the north side of this mountain.

I heard a roar of fluttering birds flying above the giant trees. They were so numerous that they shut out the sun and the forest floor was almost dark for a full five minutes. Good grief, could these birds be the extinct Passenger Pigeons?

I thought back again as to how on earth I got here with no avail for an answer. I reasoned that it was most likely late spring or early summer as to the size of leaves and numerous wild flowers blooming everywhere.

What should I do? Will I ever get back home? Why am I here, do I have a mission I wondered?

In case I am here for the rest of my life, I must prepare for the uncertain future. What will I eat? Where will I sleep? Reckon there are other human beings that live in this beautiful world?

Colonel Charles Dahnmon Whitt

Dahnmon's Fantastic Dream

Wild Indians

Just as I had that thought, my eyes caught motion coming around the hill on one of the heavily traveled traces. A faint sunbeam from the heavens cast a sparkle on something moving on the trail. Man, I could not believe my eyes. It was a party of Indian warriors heading in my direction.

I instantly knelt down behind a bush so as not to be seen. I was not prepared for such a world even though I had studied and learned all I could about early America.

Too late, the scouting Indian with his sharp eyes has seen me. The whole party was upon me in a flash so I just stood up and said "Hello, I am Dahnmon Whitt."

The Indians seemed to be as shocked at me. They surrounded me and every eye was fixed upon me. They all gazed with great curiosity and several made the deep gruntal sounds that only red men can.

Some of the Indians spoke a few words, but I had no idea of what they said. The man I figured to be the chief walked up close and touched me, but instinctively jerked his hand back. Some of the warriors snickered.

Colonel Charles Dahnmon Whitt

Dahnmon's Fantastic Dream

My fears subsided somewhat and I stuck my hand out as if to shake the chief's hand. He looked at it and then he grabbed it for a quick shake as if he didn't know what to expect.

The Indians were curious as to how I was dressed and kept looking at my shiny watch. They also loved my Kentucky gentlemen's ring with all the shiny little diamonds.

I noticed that there was nine of them with two being teen agers. The Indians were not as dark as I expected either. I guess that living in the shade of the green canopy provided by the huge trees held back the suntans.

The warriors all carried bows and arrows and war clubs all made of stone. I fixed the time before the French and English had arrived.

They all wore skin shirts and breach clothes adorned with some type of beads and animal teeth. Mostly the men had shaved hair off most of their scalps with one big yank of hair on one side adorned with eagle and turkey feathers. A couple of the warriors had full heads of hair which hung down on their shoulders. All wore moccasins and animal skin leggings.

None had painted faces so I felt relieved and knew they were not on the warpath.

Colonel Charles Dahnmon Whitt

Dahnmon's Fantastic Dream

I spoke the word, "Cherokee". One puzzled warrior answered back, "Cher-o-kee"

Nothing was settled as to whom they were, but at least I wasn't dead.

Now the chief reached out and pulled on my "T" shirt and said something. All the warriors laughed, so I laughed with them.

I did not want to show fear so I reached out and pulled the skin shirt and spoke, "nice"! He grinned at me. Now maybe we are getting somewhere I thought.

Out of the blue one of the teenaged warriors ran up and slapped me on the face and yelled something really loud.

Before I knew it I had given him a right handed fist and knocked him back and down on the ground he went.

The whole Indian party jumped back and was in attack mode. We all stood there and looked at each other for close to a minute. The chief burst out in laughter and all of us joined in. I walked up to the young man on the ground and stuck my hand out to help him up. This pleased all the warriors. The chief said something to the young warrior and laughed. The young man smiled at the chief and also me.

Colonel Charles Dahnmon Whitt

Dahnmon's Fantastic Dream

Now this is some dream, it is much too real. Is it real I wondered? Could I be dead and can this place be paradise?

What about my family? Will they know that I have gone away to this strange, but wonderful land?

What's next, will the Indians force me to go with them, or will I go with them on my own? I must plan to survive!

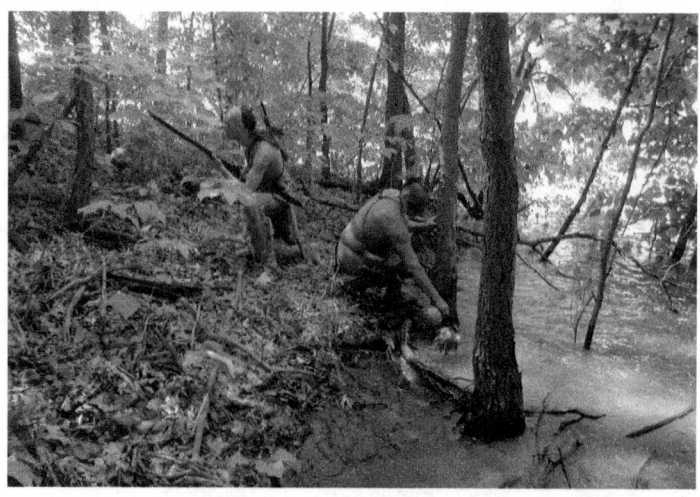

One of my new Indian friends gets water while another stands guard. That is an ever day occurrence, always careful.

Colonel Charles Dahnmon Whitt

Dahnmon's Fantastic Dream

My new Friends

The Indians became cautious friends as did I.

It looks like I am stuck here in this beautiful wilderness. I must do whatever it takes to preserve myself and survive.

Surviving and even thriving is what these Native Americans are all about. If I can win their trust and learn from them I may be able to get back home someday.

If I am not dead and I am truly here in this wilderness, I will be looking forward to leaving this paradise and going on to Heaven. This may be heaven. I am so mixed up with what's going on. I pinched myself again, Ohhhh! This is real!

The Indians have let down their guard since they see I mean them no harm. I am starting to like them, (Indians) I just need to learn to communicate with them better. A smile always helps.

The Chief spoke to two of the braves and at once they headed down to the river. . I see that they went after water and I was surprised to see that they always watch each other's back.

Colonel Charles Dahnmon Whitt

Dahnmon's Fantastic Dream

I asked the Chief what the river's name was by pointing to the river and signing as best as I could. "Pellissippi," said the Chief.

I was right this is the Clinch. I remember my research and that was the Indian name for the Clinch River. Man I am back in the area where I grew up with a little 400 years difference in time.

While the two braves were getting water the Chief told another brave something and the brave came to me and handed me some dried meat and parched corn. I presume the dried meat to be deer or elk. It is commonly referred to as "Jerky." The parched corn was what we call, "Corn Nuts," in the 21st century.

I thanked him and the Chief. I remembered I had some change in my pocket, so I dug out a quarter, a few dimes, nickels, and pennies and gave each Indian a coin. They were excited to get them and thought they must be of great value. I gave the chief the quarter; I guess I thought the higher value should go to the chief. What am I thinking; I gave the chief only 25 cents?

The braves all looked their coins over and noticed the bust of a man on each. They signed to me to give them some explanation.

Colonel Charles Dahnmon Whitt

Dahnmon's Fantastic Dream

I pointed to my head as if to say that these men on the coins were head of a country. I patted the Chief on the shoulder and said, "Chief." I think this satisfied them for now. I noticed that each tucked away their new prize into their little medicine bags.

I took out my wallet and pulled out the photo ID of my Kentucky driver's license. I showed the Chief my picture, and he just about freaked out. I guess he thought it was a spirit captured someway.

I held out my hands in a calming way to show the Chief there was nothing to fear. Before I thought I said it is my Kentucky driver's license.

"Cain-tuck-kee," said the chief.

"Yes, your hunting grounds," I said while I crunched over acting as if I had a bow and arrow drawn on some animal.

The Chief understood the word, Kentucky if nothing else. The Chief wanted my driver's license, so I gave it to him. Nothing to drive in this new world I figured. The Chief was very happy to have my picture on this funny material and also the name Kentucky spoken with it.

The Chief proudly stuck my license into his medicine bag and then he pulled out his war club. I must have looked alarmed because the Chief

Colonel Charles Dahnmon Whitt

Dahnmon's Fantastic Dream

laughed. He handed me the war club handle first as a sign of friendship.

It was a well-made fighting tool. It was a smooth stone about 5 inches long and had been grooved on the side to fit it into the handle. It was covered with animal skin. I would think that it had been stretched over the stone while it was wet. After drying the skin shrink and became very tight over the stone and handle. The handle had a nice feather attached to it with little shallow carvings all over it. It was very well built by a sixteen hundreds Native American. I wondered if it had ever been used on an enemy's skull. I was not about to try and ask that. I thanked the Chief with every sign I could come up with and he gave me a little crooked smile.

After the trade the Chief tapped his chest and said, "Co-o-nah."

He was telling me his name. I wondered what it meant. The Chief saw the puzzlement on my face so he stuck out both hands with all the fingers spread. He gently shook his hands up and down so I thought it meant rain. Then he simulated a cold winter shiver. His name must mean winter or snow. I shook my head in acknowledgement.

I tapped myself on the chest and said, Dahn-mon. Then Co-o-nah gave me a little crooked smile and grabbed my forearm in a greeting.

Colonel Charles Dahnmon Whitt

Dahnmon's Fantastic Dream

The other warriors wanted to know about their coins.

I said, "Presidents!"

I said Co-o-nah is president to try and explain the president as a chief like Co-o-nah.
I pointed to Chief Co-o-nah and said president. They looked back and said, "Hah-Hah."

I took it to mean yes.

Co-o-nah spoke and the other Indians were ready to travel. Next Co-o-nah motioned for me to join them so I got in line behind one of the braves and he turned and smiled with approval.

Here I was living in the sixteen hundreds and in getting ready to travel with a party of Indians.

Where would we go and what will we be doing?

I wish my family could see me now. I always wanted to be an Indian and now I guess I am.

Colonel Charles Dahnmon Whitt

Dahnmon's Fantastic Dream
Traveling Indian Style

Co-o-nah spoke a word or two and a brave went out in front about twenty yards and the march began. The brave out front was the point guard and the one that had spotted me in the woods.

We were basically heading northwest up the Pellissippi, (Clinch River). I think we were in the area of what is now Raven, Virginia. The river looked the same, but different. It was full of clear water and was about double its size as I remember it in 2012. We just passed the mouth of Mill Creek, where I grew up. There were no roads or railroads as was the case in 2012.

The next place I recognized was what we called the "Curve" It was a steep bend in the river where I had swam as a boy, yes back in the nineteen-hundreds. We were on the left side of the river and I could see the bottom land across the river. This is where Raven school was built back in the late nineteen-fifties.

The bottom was covered with the giant trees, but I could see pretty far through the clear forest floor.

The Indians didn't fool around while traveling; they set a demanding pace for this old paleface. I kept up without complaining so they were pleased with me.

Colonel Charles Dahnmon Whitt

Dahnmon's Fantastic Dream

Next we traveled up to the mouth of a creek that is now called Coal Creek. This is the place where the little town of Raven, VA is now located.

The brave out front as I called the point guard was setting the pace and looking in all directions as we traveled. The Clinch was like a snake that moved back and forth across the valley floor.

Next we passed the mouth of what is now Mud Lick Creek. After that the Clinch moved toward the other side of the valley. This is where the point guard veered away from the river and headed on a trail up the left side of the of the Clinch Valley.

We must be heading to a specific location I surmised.

We crossed another creek; this is what we call Hill Creek today.

Up ahead there was a hill and many trails and evidence of people being about. We went up a rise and I realized that there was an Indian town here. I could see Wigwais (Indian lodges) circled about on the hill. I saw a big long house in the center of the Indian town. I saw smoke coming up from the cooking fires and heard the sounds of children playing. Next we saw a brave up in a tree signing our party to come on in and a boy runner headed to

Colonel Charles Dahnmon Whitt

Dahnmon's Fantastic Dream

the big Long House that had to be their council house.

I remembered that the Clinch Valley Hospital was built on this hill in the 20th century. They called it Town Hill and had found evidence that Indians had lived there back in time. As a matter of fact I was born in that hospital on this same little hill.

As we entered the Indian Town the women and children ran to meet us. I noticed that some of the women were greeting their husbands from the trip.

Next, I was the main attraction as the curiosity grew. I was a sight that none of these people had ever seen.

I could not help but notice that most of the children were naked and most of the women were bare breasted with something like panty looms from their waist down. I tried not to gaze, but I was seeing some strange sights among my Indian friends.

Co-o-nah led us into the town and right up to the Longhouse or Council House. He looked at me and said, "mis-kah-mi-qui."
I took it to mean a place of importance where the people's decisions are made.

Colonel Charles Dahnmon Whitt

Dahnmon's Fantastic Dream

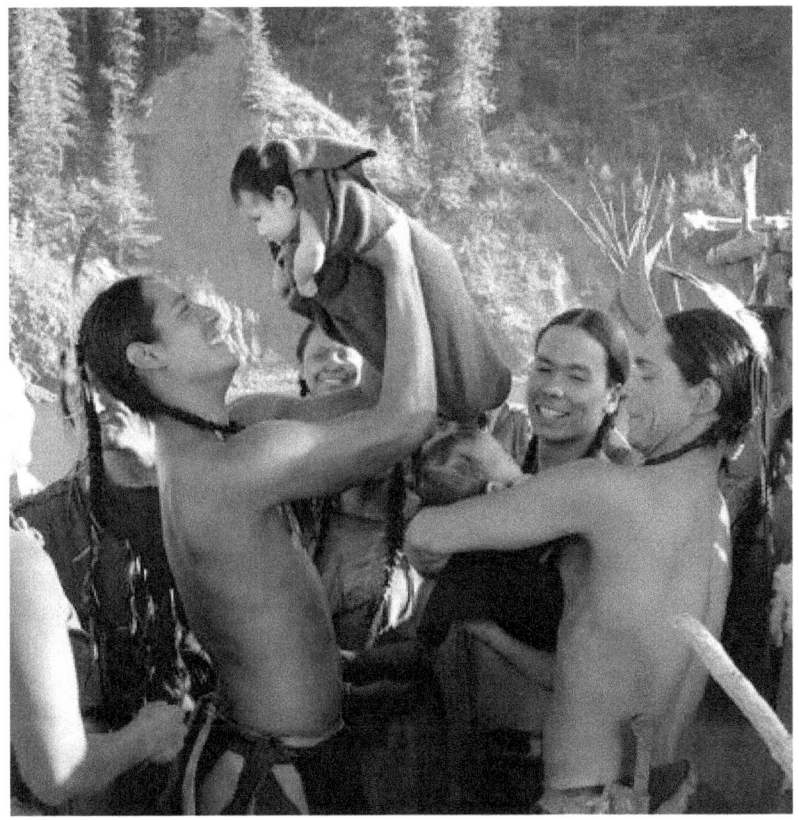

Family reunion after the braves return from a mission.

Colonel Charles Dahnmon Whitt

Dahnmon's Fantastic Dream

We stood by the Council House door and waited for the Chief inside to have his report from Co-o-nah. Evidently not everyone is invited into the presence of the main Chief or venture into the Council House.

Next, after about a 20 minute wait Co-o-nah came out and said something. Then he looked at me and said, "Kitchokema." He signed that he was a Chief but Kitchokema meant a greater Chief. He signed that this Chief was named for the Panther. Meshepeshe was the word for Panther.

I was uneasy to meet this Panther Chief. I hope he does not live up to his name.

A brave with all kinds of paint on him and decorated in many colors came to the door and beckoned for us to come in and meet the Panther Chief.

Colonel Charles Dahnmon Whitt

Dahnmon's Fantastic Dream

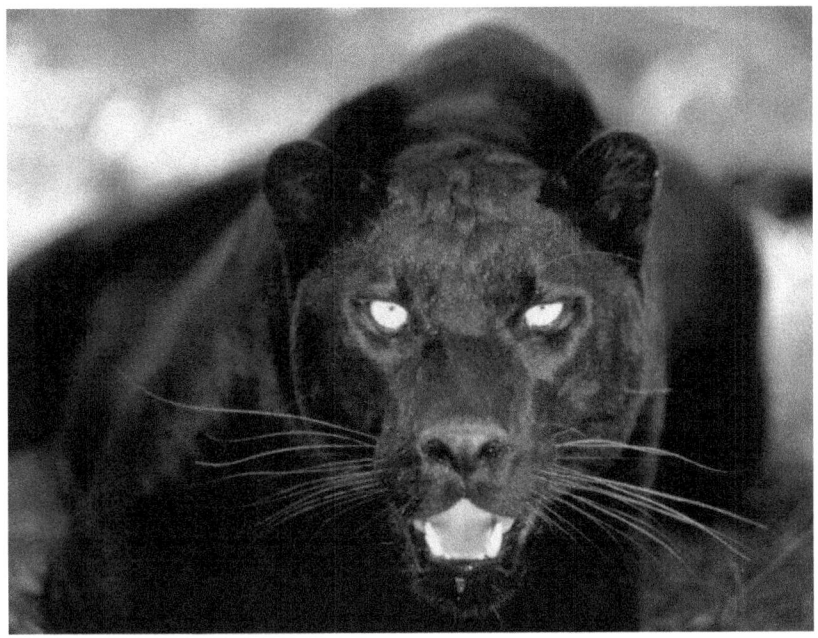

This is what I thought the great Chief; "Panther" might be like.

Colonel Charles Dahnmon Whitt

Dahnmon's Fantastic Dream

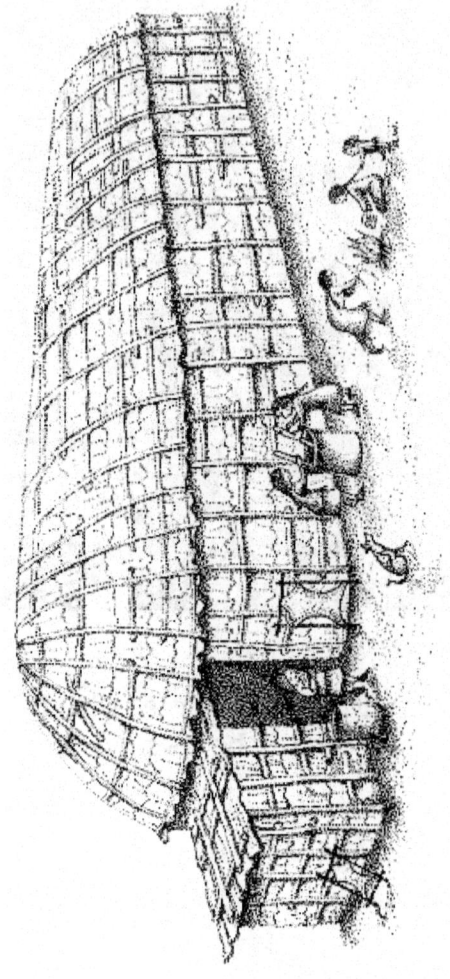

Council House

Colonel Charles Dahnmon Whitt

Dahnmon's Fantastic Dream

I Meet The Panther

Meshepshe has received his report and he was very anxious to meet this white man with funny clothes and carries a funny card with his spirit on it and speaks of Cain-Tuc-Kee.

Meshepshe did not wait; he rose to his feet and welcomed me. He came right to me as I entered the Council House.

He laughed with glee as he looked me over, so I started laughing also. First thing I knew the whole of the Indians were laughing.

He had seen my Kentucky driver's license by now and heard of the coins I had given the braves. He held up the quarter that I had given to Co-o-nah and looked at me as if to ask, "Where's mine?"

I had no more change so I took out my wallet and got a dollar out. I handed it to the Panther and he took it with a smile. He then looked at me for an explanation.

"It's President Washington," I said.
I went through the whole routine signing that Washington was like a Kitchokema. This pleased the Panther.

Colonel Charles Dahnmon Whitt

Dahnmon's Fantastic Dream

He looked at me and studied my face and my glasses. He looked me up and down and smiled again. He took his dollar and tucked it away into a pouch.

I had to show him my little Case knife. I opened the blade and showed the chief how sharp it was. I could see he wanted it, but I would not volunteer to give it to him as I may need it to survive here.

The Panther wanted to see my watch, so I took it off and handed it to him. As he concentrated on it he saw the second hand sweeping around the face of the watch. His almost black eyes widened and he handed it back to me. I think the Panther thought it was alive or possessed a spirit.

The Panther held out his arms as if to say, "What is it?"

I signed the best way I could to tell him that it kept track of the sun which told me the time.

The Panther laughed again and signed that they had no need for such a thing, they had the sun.

I smiled at the Chief.

It was getting late in the day and the shadows of the great trees were bringing on darkness.

Colonel Charles Dahnmon Whitt

Dahnmon's Fantastic Dream

The Panther turned to Co-o-nah and gave him instructions.

The Panther took my forearm as a sign of peace and sent me following Co-o-nah.

I followed Co-o-nah to a wigewa and we entered. He motioned for me to sit down on some furs and then he told a squaw something. She left and was soon back with a wooden bowl of some type of meaty stew and something like cornbread, but it was flat with no rise.

He told me to eat and explained the best that he could that something would happen in the morning after the sun rises. He also signed that I must be very brave. I had no idea what it would be, but I was ready to eat so I eat the food and lay down on the furs.

I noticed that there was a warrior stationed outside my door. Was he there to keep me there or to protect me?

I had had a busy day and was concerned about all that has transpired that day. I wondered what was supposed to happen to me in the morning. I didn't wonder long, I was so tired that I fell asleep quickly.

Colonel Charles Dahnmon Whitt

Dahnmon's Fantastic Dream
A Dream Within A Dream

As I slept I could see that I was in a hospital and doctors and nurses were standing around me.

What now I thought?

I was having a dream now what, a dream within a dream? Reckon I have been out of my head, I wondered.

No, the Indians and my visit with them was just too real to be a dream.

I heard a doctor say, he has good brain impulses. I think he will come out of it eventually. We just need to keep him stable and nourished.

I heard my preacher praying and my family looked so forlorn.

I tried to speak to them! I could think it but they couldn't hear me.
"People, I am fine, I just need to sleep a little longer," I pleaded.

I just couldn't make a sound or move a muscle.

I wonder if I am paralyzed, was my thought?

Colonel Charles Dahnmon Whitt

Dahnmon's Fantastic Dream

I began to come and go out of consciousness.

The next thing I knew I was out like a light again and on my way back to the primitive days of 1600.

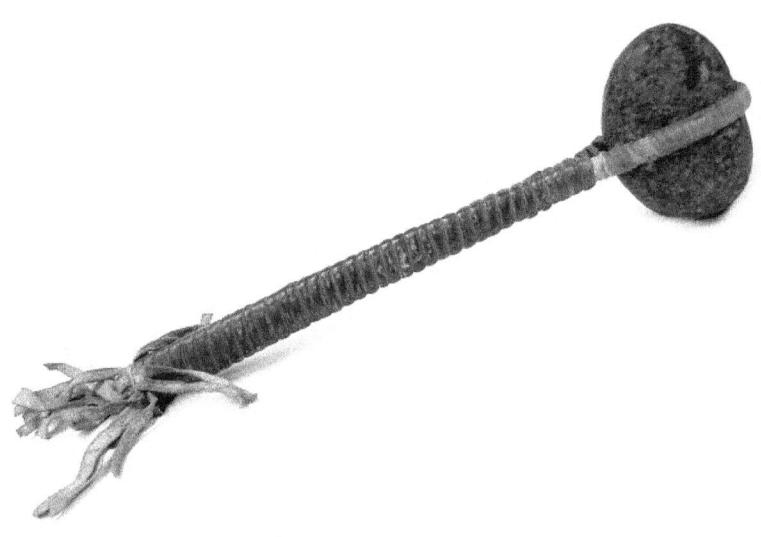

Indian War Club

Colonel Charles Dahnmon Whitt

Dahnmon's Fantastic Dream
The Gauntlet And A Bath.

I went back to sleep and the next thing I knew it was morning. I could see the new day sun shining around my door and I could hear commotion outside my lodge.

Just as I was thinking about getting up, five braves came in and pulled me to my feet. This really alarmed me.

Before I could get a word out, they were pulling off all my clothes. They took off every stitch of clothes I had including my shoes and socks. One of the Indians thought that my little sport socks were funny and laughed as he threw them to the ground.

Next I was pulled out of the lodge bare naked. I looked out across the village and saw two lines of folks. The lines were parallel and were made up of 70 to 80 people including the women and children. They were all excited to see me and were wielding a switch. I didn't see any one holding a club which was good news.

I have always heard of these gauntlets but never dreamed I would be running one until now.

Co-o-nah came to my side and held me by my arm and pointed down the long lines of people. At the

Colonel Charles Dahnmon Whitt

Dahnmon's Fantastic Dream

end was the Council House where the Panther was standing.

Co-o-nah signed to me, that if I fell, to get up quickly and run hard to the Kitchokema. Be brave, he signified.

Nothing to do but take off and run hard keeping my feet under me, so without notice I sprinted past the first couple of swinging switches.

Ooooh! I was on fire with the stinging of the switches and the squaws were laughing at my naked body being whipped with the switches. Even the little children got a lick on me more times than I can count. It seemed like an eternity, but I was soon at The Council house being greeted by the Panther. He was pleased that I had run bravely through the gauntlet.

I was standing there naked and had whelps rising up all over my body. Before I could say a word, six squaws accompanied by Co-o-nah were grabbing me. I thought I would have to run it again.

Co-o-nah motioned for me to go with them.

"Hey, I'm naked," I said as I was being pulled toward the river.

Colonel Charles Dahnmon Whitt

Dahnmon's Fantastic Dream

The squaws were all laughing as they pulled me on across the long bottom to the Clinch.

They kept saying something that I couldn't understand. I got the gist of it I think; they were going to wash me in the river.

We came to the river and I was taken out to a part of the river which had a sandy, gravely bottom.
The squaws were mostly middle aged I thought, but one was a beautiful young woman. They were all bare breasted and the biggest squaw jumped high and down on me to duck me down into the water. I came out gasping for air but they all were rubbing me with the sand and gravel.

"My word, I am going to be nothing but raw meat," I exclaimed.

They laughed and kept scrubbing me with the grit. We were all close together and I think that some of the women were getting scrubbed some also.

They finally let up and I was as red as a redbird. They begin to rub me with their bare hands and saying something that I could not understand.

Finally one pointed to herself and then to me. I first thought Oh! No., but realized that they were making a Redman out of me so I could be one of them.

Colonel Charles Dahnmon Whitt

Dahnmon's Fantastic Dream

I was really backward about being naked in front of
the women and even the whole town, but now I gave
up and just strutted back to town as if I had all my
clothes on.
Co-o-nah met me at the edge of the town and I could
see he was pleased with me.

The squaws kept me in tow and took me to a lodge
and sat me down on a bear rug. They all gathered
around and they all gently rubbed something
soothing on every part of my body. The sting left and
I could actually feel my body beginning to heal. I
think it was bear grease with some secret herbs
mixed in.

Next a soft doeskin shirt was put on me and then
they pulled me to my feet. A breach cloth was pulled
between my legs and held up in front and back
while a belt was fastened around my waist. Then a
pair of moccasins were put on my feet and laced up
on to my ankles.

The squaws were finished and all giggled their way
out of the lodge.

Colonel Charles Dahnmon Whitt

Dahnmon's Fantastic Dream
Mutual Respect

I begin to feel much better after such a trying morning. The gauntlet and the scrubbing in the Clinch River were quite an ordeal.

The salve of bear grease and herbs were working wonders, I had very little pain even though I was so pink.

Co-o-nah was well pleased with my performance in the gauntlet. I do know that this was a very mild gauntlet compared to some I have read about. I think that the Panther and Co-o-nah must have really liked me. The men in the lines did not swing clubs as they often do. They can do a lot of damage to the human body. Clubs can break bones and damage vital organs. I have heard of men being beaten totally to death. If you fall and don't jump back up they consider that a sign of weakness and really beat you then.

I was now a respected citizen of the Indian village. I was very respectful of these red people.

The Indians allowed me freedom to walk about and visit all of the people even thought we could not communicate too well.

Colonel Charles Dahnmon Whitt

Dahnmon's Fantastic Dream

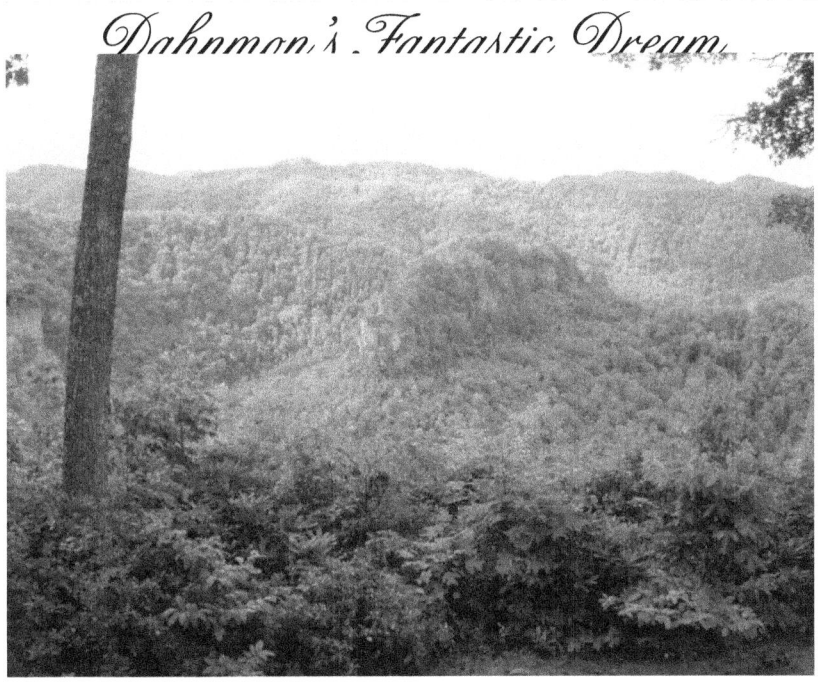

The beautiful Mountains of South-West Virginia.
This is the Breaks of the Russell

Colonel Charles Dahnmon Whitt

Dahnmon's Fantastic Dream

Challenges

The young braves are always trying to show their manhood and talents of an Indian brave.

Some of the young braves brought their bows and arrows and challenged me to a shooting match. I am sure they thought I would look bad and they would look good.

The young braves had no idea that I had shot arrows many times as a teenager and actually hunted with a bow in the late twentieth century.

The archery equipment of the Indians was not near as sophisticated as the modern bows of the twentieth century, but I would be able to hold my own. The Indians depended more on stealth than the quality of their bows and arrows.

I noticed that the young man gave me the most crooked arrow in his quiver. I looked it over and stuck it back and got one that would fly straighter.

He looked at me but never said anything. The young men had set up a big chunk of bark and had all hit it with an arrow, but none had hit it in the center.

It was my time so I drew back the bow and let my arrow fly straight to the center of the target.

Colonel Charles Dahnmon Whitt

Dahnmon's Fantastic Dream

The young braves all cheered for me even thought I
had beaten them. The young brave that gave me the
bow and arrow was amazed and gave me a little
crocked smile.

I noticed Co-o-nah had been standing a few yards
away observing the whole thing. He gave me a look
of approval when my arrow had hit the mark.

The young warriors all liked me, but were always
trying to show me up by their skills. The next thing
that came up was the fire building session. All the
braves carried flint to build there fires.

They all gathered around with me the closest to the
young man that was going to demonstrate the fire
building by flint. He got some nice tinder and a
dried mushroom to catch the spark and placed it on
the ground on top of the tinder. After three strikes a
spark caught in the dried mushroom and he picked
it up and gently blew into it. Then fire began to
flame up from the tiny spark.

I cheered for him and patted him on the head as he
was still squatted with his little flame growing. He
dropped it on the ground and patted out the fire.

Next he looked at me as a challenge. I looked back
and borrowed his stone knife. I looked around the
edge of the town for some soft wood. I saw just what

Colonel Charles Dahnmon Whitt

Dahnmon's Fantastic Dream

I needed. There was a patch of yucca with some dead but dry spindles still there from last year. I picked me a nice straight one about ¾ of an inch in diameter and cut it free. Next I walked about looking for a split piece of soft but dry wood. I found a piece of red wood about 3 inches wide and about ¾ of an inch thick. I got some bark-tinder from a cedar tree. I walked back over and squatted with the young men. I cut a point on the spindle, and then I started a hole about ¾ of an inch from the edge of the redwood. I cut a notch from the edge to the hole. I made myself a top out of another piece of wood. I borrowed a bow from one of the young braves. I was ready. I laid the redwood down on the tinder with the notch just about in the center of the tender. I took the spindle and twisted into the rawhide bow string set the sharp end in the partially drilled hole. I put the top with a hole in it on top of the spindle. I let out a long breath of air and went to work pulling the bow back and forth briskly and the spindle was spinning fast. It only took about 45 seconds and the smoke was pouring up. I could see the little red ember I had created with the bow and spindle. I bumped out the amber on the tender and picked it up and gently blew oxygen on to the amber. I had all that was required for a fire. I had fuel, heat, and oxygen. The little flame appeared and the crowd of boys and men cheered for me.

I found that these folks had never seen it done with a bow. They took a small stick and used their hands

Colonel Charles Dahnmon Whitt

Dahnmon's Fantastic Dream

to build a fire. That had to take much patience. I think I had improved on their method of building fire by friction.

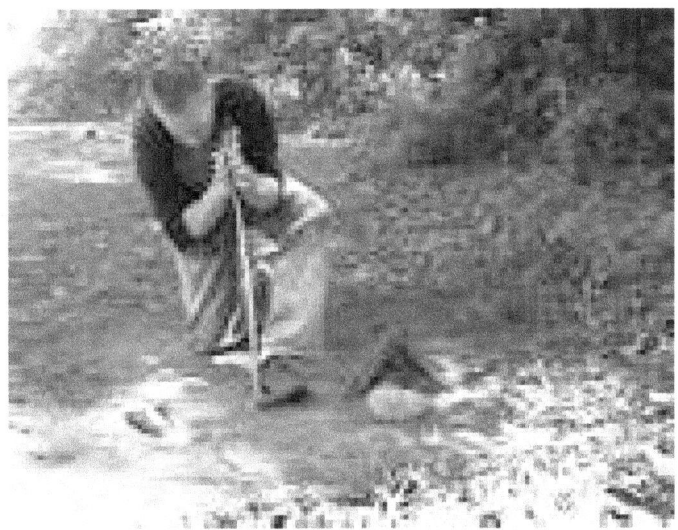

Indian Style in the East Woodland.

Colonel Charles Dahnmon Whitt

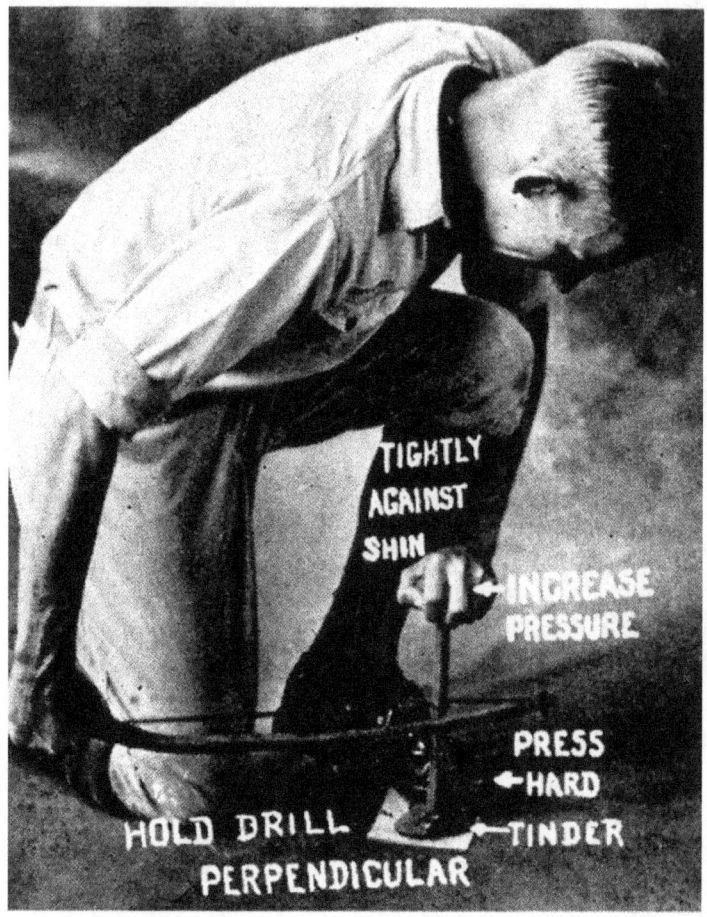

Dahnmon's Fantastic Dream

My style I taught the Indians.

I learned this in the Boy Scouts.

Colonel Charles Dahnmon Whitt

Dahnmon's Fantastic Dream

Squaw

Co-o-nah had been observing me ever since I joined them. He was looking out for me and he made me feel really welcome with his people.

He brought a nice looking squaw to me and signed that she was mine.

I was startled and signed back that I did not need a woman; I have one I explained the best way I could.

Co-o-nah was surprised and puzzled. In his world a man could have as many squaws as he could take care of.

I finally got my point across even though he probably thought I had ED as some older men have that problem. At any rate it worked, but he still insisted that I keep her to take care of my other needs such as food, shelter, and so-on.

He had patted his belly and pointed to his mouth and chewed as to tell me she would be a good cook for me. I think he believed I needed a helper and living here in 1600 I think he was right.

I agreed to let her be my helper. Her name was Raven and I could remember this for two reasons. I was raised in Raven, Virginia in the 1950's and the

Colonel Charles Dahnmon Whitt

Dahnmon's Fantastic Dream

other reason was that her hair was as black as a raven.

We had little to do with each other at first as I felt she was just in the way until I got hungry. I found out that she was very handy to have around. Raven tried to get into my bed with me the first night, but I made it clear she could not. I figured she would be just too much temptation for me if she slept with me. She learned to sleep by herself on her own bearskin rug.

I was thinking how proud my wife would be of my character if I ever get back to tell her.

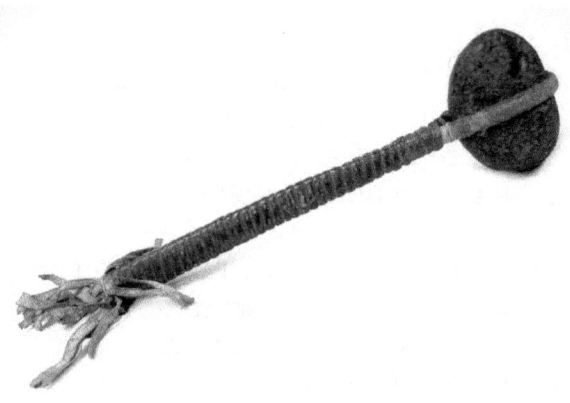

Indian War Club

Colonel Charles Dahnmon Whitt

Dahnmon's Fantastic Dream

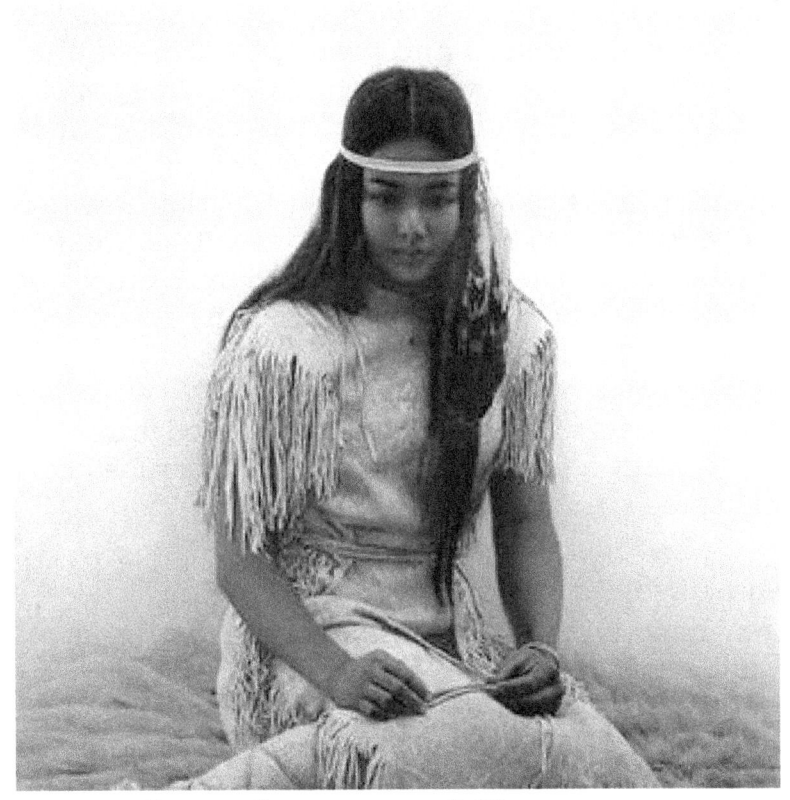

Rendition of Raven

Colonel Charles Dahnmon Whitt

Dahnmon's Fantastic Dream

My first Hunt

I had been in the Indian village on Town Hill for about two weeks now and I was getting use to the idea of living this new life. Of course I thought of getting back home every time I had an idle minute.

One morning as I ate whatever it was that Raven had given me; Co-o-nah came to me with a dozen braves ready for a hunt. He handed me a quiver of arrows and a bow. I already carried my prized war club.

Raven observed this and ran into the lodge and brought out a pouch filled with jerky, parched corn, and some kind dried fruit.

Now I Wore buckskin leggings up past my knees, a breach cloth but I kept my Sketcher running shoes. I had a soft buckskin shirt on. I also wore a coonskin hat with the tail hanging down like Davy Crockett wore on the television series. The Indians were amused at my oddities.

By now I knew I was going out with a party of hunters. I was anxious to get out and see some more territory anyway.

We followed the Clinch River upstream this time. We did not go in a rush this time and it was like before

Colonel Charles Dahnmon Whitt

Dahnmon's Fantastic Dream

when they took me to their town; none of the braves made any unnecessary noise. Also we had a point guard about twenty yards ahead to watch for trouble.

We traveled to a great saltlick at the end of a mountain. I remember this area from the twenty-first century, it is called Paint Lick.

We came in from the down-wind side and stalked up a hill and crawled to the summit of the hill so we could view the saltlick.

I could hardly believe what my eyes could see. There were hundreds of animals enjoying the salt lick. There was a great herd of elk, a vast number of deer, and even some buffalo.

I looked over to the brave beside me and he looked back with a big smile on his face. I guess he could see my wide eyes and expression of disbelief.

Co-o-nah backs down the hill and we all do likewise. He wanted to get us out of sight and sound of the grazing and licking herds.

He gave the instructions as to how the hunt would go. Co-o-nah signed for me to stick with him.

It was amazing to watch the skill and organization of the hunting braves. They Indians spread out in

Colonel Charles Dahnmon Whitt

Dahnmon's Fantastic Dream

pairs and they all had dear skins with the hair still on and they covered their heads and backs as a camouflage to fool the quarry. All the hunters carried their bows with a flint rock arrow notched and ready to release.

It was determined that the first brave that had a good shot would take the shot. Only one brave in each pair would shoot.

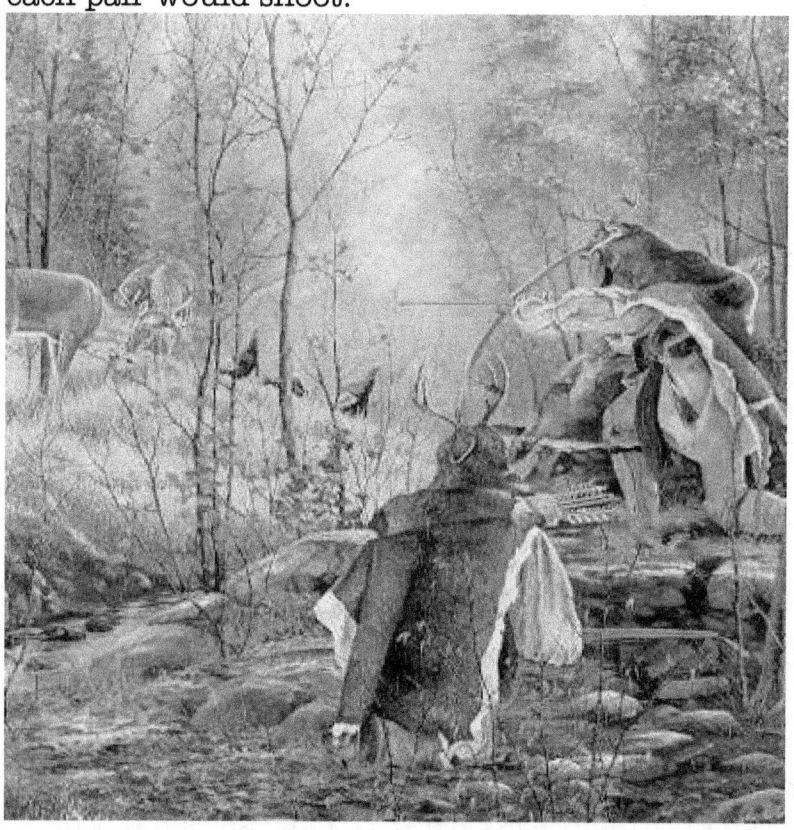

Colonel Charles Dahnmon Whitt

Dahnmon's Fantastic Dream

Indian Style Hunting.

Every arrow hit the mark and now two elk and four deer ran a short distance and lay down and went to sleep as the life blood drained from their bodies.

The hunters were quiet and very patient as they waited. They did not want to cause a stampede or scare the other animals.

After a sufficient time the pairs of hunters went to their kill. The deer and elk were all dragged back across the hill and all went back to drag the much bigger elk across the hill.

The hunters did not want to field dress their kill so close to the lick as this may be a hindrance on other hunts. After all the animals were field-dressed and skinned, and all the lower legs removed, the meat was cut up into manageable pieces and loaded into the skins which served as packs.

Some of the hunters cut out the hearts of their kill and lifted it over their heads as a thank you to the Great Spirit. Next the hunters took a bite of the warm hearts as a sign that they had overcome a quarry and the good things of the animals would come into the hunter's body.

Colonel Charles Dahnmon Whitt

Dahnmon's Fantastic Dream

Now the work began for me. There were thirteen of us and we all took a pack of meat on our backs and headed back toward Town Hill in single file.

I was thinking how efficient the Indian hunters were and how we almost got more meat than we could carry. I noticed that the Indians never kill more than they could use.

We traveled single file with our precious load of cargo, meant to sustain the lives of these noble people. We traveled until almost dusk and came up on the camp fires of our people that came to meet us half-way. I was not expecting this but it had been prearranged.

There were no congratulations for the hunters and all was pleasant and cordial. The meeting party had fully expected us with a big load of meat for the town.

There were Indians of both sexes. They had come to meet the hunting party and to help us back to Town Hill. (Now Richlands, VA.)

Colonel Charles Dahnmon Whitt

Dahnmon's Fantastic Dream

Bull Elk
The Indian Staple.

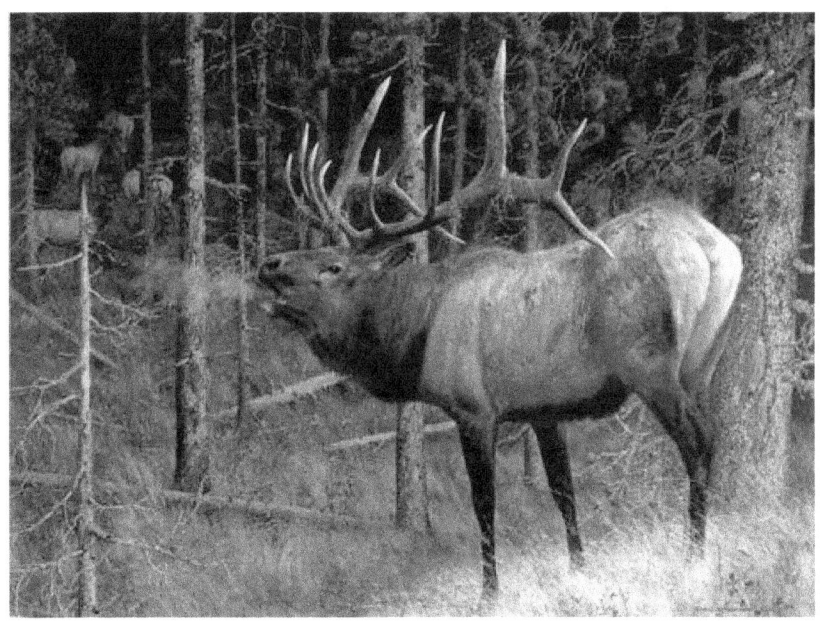

Colonel Charles Dahnmon Whitt

Dahnmon's Fantastic Dream

Learning About My Red People

I sure was glad to see our people. There I said it, "Our People". I was fitting in as if I would live my life out here among this new family of mine.

There were temporary shelters built and lots of firewood gathered.

Some of the meat would be cooked while much of it would be hung on high limbs to drain and dry.

As it began to get dark in the deep woods, many yellow eyes were all around our camp. Co-o-nah pointed to the woods with a sweeping motion of his arm. The fires about our camp were reflecting the eyes of many wolves.

Co-o-nah pointed to the fires and let me know all was well as long as we kept the fires burning. That was the purpose of big camp fires to keep these predators at bay. The wolf packs wanted our meat.

I was appointed to keep watch for the first part of the night. I felt it was an honor, but I admit I was braver on the outside than on the inside

Colonel Charles Dahnmon Whitt

Dahnmon's Fantastic Dream

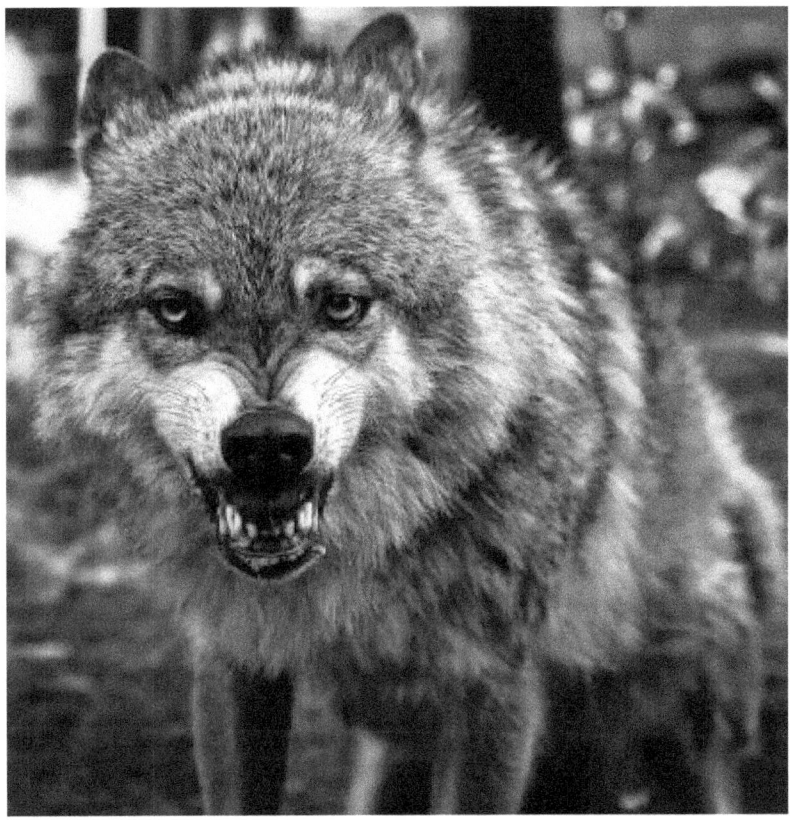

Hungry Wolf

I was joined by a young brave to watch over the sleeping people and keep the fires going strong. Every time I put wood on the fire the young brave waved and put wood on the fires he was tending. We both kept out bows and war clubs handy.

Colonel Charles Dahnmon Whitt

Dahnmon's Fantastic Dream

While I served my time on watch I noticed the eyes moving about, but none made a move to come into the camp.

I was really glad to see the morning light filtering through the deep woods as the new day dawned.

The trip back to Town Hill was uneventful and we were back by early afternoon because of all the help. There were no slackers in this party.

Every so often when I was alone in the quiet, I would think of my home back in the 21st century. How did I get here and how if ever would I get back?

I would just have to continue my course of action of just fitting in and live the life I now live. I sure didn't want to get scalped while living here in the early sixteen-hundreds, even though that may be the way I get back home. For now this is home.

I still marvel at my surroundings and the life of these noble red people. They seem so happy and go lucky. They have no shame or modesty as to how they dress or what they wear.

If you need to get up at night to go pee, you just go find a tree at the edge of the town. It is nothing to see a brave at another tree or a squaw squatting to relieve herself. No one bothers others in their lodges. I have heard love making going on and

Colonel Charles Dahnmon Whitt

Dahnmon's Fantastic Dream

happiness all around. Nothing is said, as that is part of life.

The men pick the wives in a dance and the women joins the man and they dance chest to chest with never using their arms. It is quiet an exciting dance as both parties become aroused.

The little boys receive little discipline as the Indians did not want to break their spirits.

I have noticed that the women are real farmers. They grow the biggest corn I have ever seen. I am not exaggerating when I say there were ears of corn nearly two feet long. The ground is rich and the men bring the women little fish caught from the Clinch, to put into each hill of corm. Also the beans and melons and squash are huge.

The men have it made as their duties are to hunt, fish, and guard the welfare of the people. I think they mostly have fun.

While we were at our temporary camp, two hunters went out and got our breakfast. Yes we had meat, but turkey for breakfast went really well.

Colonel Charles Dahnmon Whitt

Dahnmon's Fantastic Dream

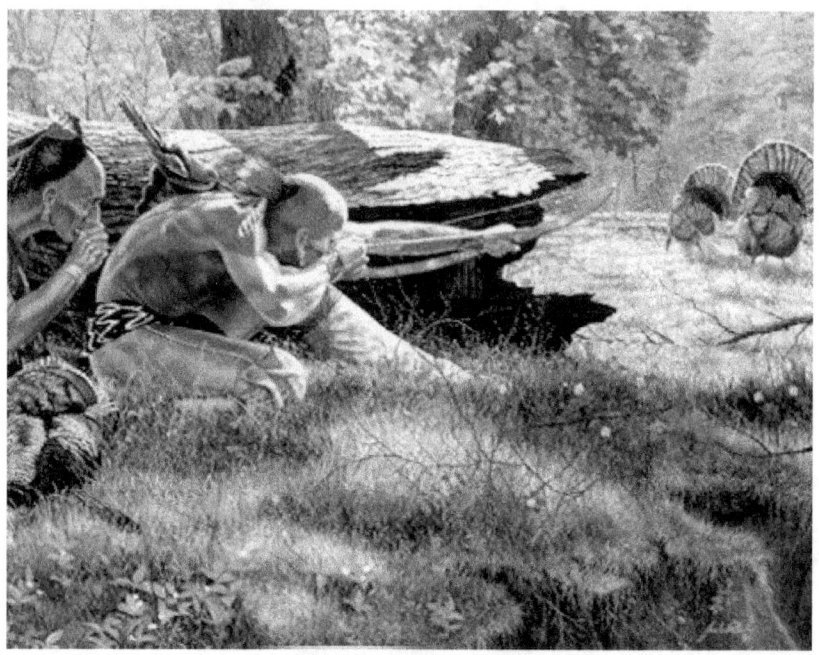

Turkey Hunters

I have finally figured out the tribe I live with. The Shawnee lived on the east coast for many years and have moved about. They will eventually settle in the Ohio country. This group is a forward sect of that tribe.

My Indians were a branch of the Shawnee that had moved from the east in the past 5 years or so. They later would make homes north of the Ohio River and would come to Virginia and Kentucky to hunt.

Colonel Charles Dahnmon Whitt

Dahnmon's Fantastic Dream

The Shawnee Indians, also of Algonquian stock, lived in the east. Their first contact with white men came in the 1600s. Early estimates of their population range from 3,000 to 50,000, although 10,000 appear to be the most probable estimate. Shawnee comes from the Algonquian word 'Shawun' (shawunogi) meaning 'southerner.' The application of southerner is indicative of their location compared to the other Algonquian tribes who lived to the Shawnee's north, around the Great Lakes.

I spoke the word Shaw-nee and my friends smiled proudly and tapped their chests.

Colonel Charles Dahnmon Whitt

Dahnmon's Fantastic Dream
The Savage Side

I was sitting around the campfire one afternoon when a commotion arose at the edge of Town Hill. All the people ran to the edge of the town to meet the returning scouts. They had two strange Indians in tow with leather ropes around their necks and their hands tied in the back. They had been treated pretty rough from the way they looked. All they wore was their breech cloths and moccasins. They both had long hair with no decorations of any kind. I presume they had been stripped of everything.

The leader of the scouting party headed straight to the Council House to give a report to the Panther.

The others in charge of the captives took them to a tree and threw the ropes over a limb and pulled it tight until the captives were stretched tight and could hardly move. The town's people all stood around and gazed at the two intruders. Some of the squaws took switches to their bare backs and legs. Some of the little boys urinated on them in a way to disgrace the two.

This is a side of the Shawnee I hadn't seen, but of course I had read of such things back in the future.

As I watched, I figured these young warriors were intruders from the south and had been caught

Colonel Charles Dahnmon Whitt

Dahnmon's Fantastic Dream

infringing on the Shawnee hunting grounds. They would not stand for that because it took food from the mouths of their people.

From what I could gather the intruders were caught near the mountain called Paint Lick near the salt lick.

The Panther walked casually to where the two captives were tied. He looked at them and all the other people stood back so he could come close. He shouted some strong words at them, none I understood. I would guess he was telling them they made one big mistake coming to his hunting grounds.

I could see fear in the eyes of the two young men, even thought they were putting up a good front to look brave.

The chief turned to the people and shouted a word that I totally understood, "Gauntlet."

Instantly two lines began to form from the tree to the Council House where the chief was headed to wait and watch.

This time the gauntlet included war clubs and long hard poles in the two long lines.

Colonel Charles Dahnmon Whitt

Dahnmon's Fantastic Dream

I was spoken to by one of the young braves and I knew what he wanted. I found me a switch and joined in one of the lines. No one said anything as I joined in with only a switch, they knew I would show mercy because that is the way I ran it.

I wondered if these men would be set free if they made it to the Council House. The two intruders were both good specimens of a healthy brave. They were to be one run at a time so before the warrior was ready he was shoved violently into the malay of swinging clubs and sticks.

The two were knock off their feet more than once, yet they scampered to their feet and continued. The warrior leading the race through the gauntlet was hit so hard he fell to the ground and was not moving, the other one saw this as a chance to go on to the Council House so he jumped him in the confusion. The man on the ground was now being beaten by those that could get close enough to get a lick in. The runner that made it to the Council House was being held by two strong tribesmen.

My heart went out to the young man that was lying on the ground and being beaten.

Chief Panther raised his hand and the people backed off the victim. He lay there in a fetal position and incredibly he moved his legs. He was bruised and bent but alive. I wondered what would happen next.

Colonel Charles Dahnmon Whitt

Dahnmon's Fantastic Dream

Two warriors ran to the man and jerked him to his feet. He stood on his own two feet which was incredible to me.

I thought, "Lord have mercy!"

Chief Panther gave an order and the two lines began to form again as the young warrior was taken to the start of the line to make another run.

I had little faith that the young man would be able to make the run again.

With self-preservation and adrenaline flowing, the young man took off through the line which caught many of the beaters by surprise. Somehow some way he stayed on his feet and walked up to the Panther. The Panther was pleased at the bravery of this young enemy.

The two beaten warriors were escorted to a lodge by a swarm of squaws to be ministered to. I am sure the wounds were being cleaned and the bear grease poultice was being applied.

I was proud of the two young intruders for their bravery. I have never witnessed such bravery in either of my lives.

What will they do to these two next was my next thought. I thought they should let them go, but I

Colonel Charles Dahnmon Whitt

Dahnmon's Fantastic Dream

had no idea what Chief Panther was thinking. I know that intruding in on the Shawnee hunting grounds is a huge crime for these people.

Some Buffalo were in the Virginia Mountains

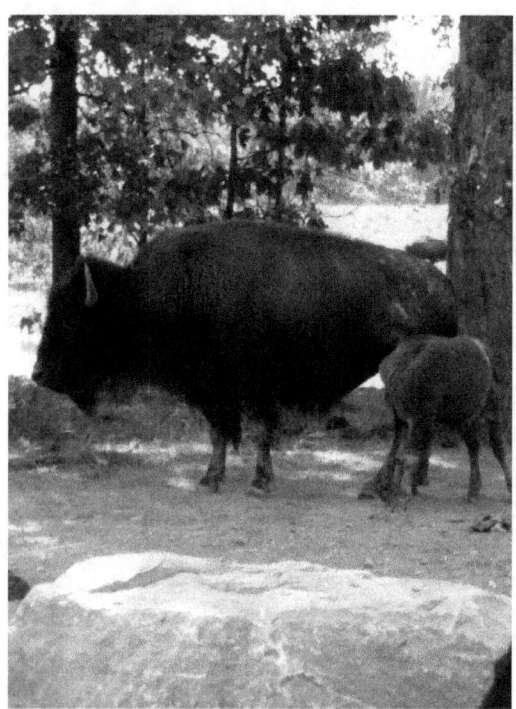

Colonel Charles Dahnmon Whitt

Dahnmon's Fantastic Dream
Tortured Beyond Belief

After watching this horrific gauntlet I sure was glad that the Panther and Co-o-nah had mercy on me and only allowed switched when I ran my gauntlet?

The Indian village on Town Hill became quiet and everyone went about their business.

The two young intruders from the Cherokee or Creek tribe had hunted in the Shawnee hunting grounds and had paid a price, but it was not all settled as yet.

The two intruders had been tied in an unnatural position with their feet back on their rump and their hands tied behind them to their feet. They also had a noose around their necks and tied tight to a branch to impede movement. Also two strong warriors had guarded the two closely.

In the morning the two were untied and brought to sit in front of a camp fire and squaws brought them good food. I was amazed at this token of goodwill. They stretched out their aching muscles and the healing salve had already begun to work on the many cuts and bruises.

Colonel Charles Dahnmon Whitt

Dahnmon's Fantastic Dream

After the two had hastily eaten the food, Chief Panther came and stood before them. The two men rose to their feet in honor of the Chief authority.

"Lord have mercy, the chief screamed words at the two that a fly wouldn't land on. I don't know what he said but the whole village cheered and the two southern braves seemed to understand.

The Indian brave that had made it through the gauntlet was taken to a lodge, not by squaws but by four strong braves, and the other was made to sit in front of the Council House.

In a short time the warrior emerged from the lodge and was painted black. The warriors that had taken him had made paint of charcoal and grease; he now was black. This was the mark of death administered as a penalty for hunting in the Shawnee hunting grounds. I remember this sign in my studies of the Indians.

He was taken to a tree. His wrists were bound with long rawhide thongs. The thongs were cast over a limb and soon the young victim was hanging by his wrists, with his free feet about a foot off the ground. This had to be very painful.

I noticed that some torches had been brought to a campfire closest to the painted warrior. I wondered what purpose the torches would play, if they were

Colonel Charles Dahnmon Whitt

Dahnmon's Fantastic Dream

going to burn him there would be plenty of firewood brought up. There was no firewood.

There he hung, naked, painted black and the tight rawhide thongs cut into his wrists.

The other warrior that had been sitting at the Council House was brought forward so he could see every detail.

The painted man said not a word, but he did have a noticeable frown on his face caused by the pain.

The tom, tom, tom of the drum made an eerie sound as the young Shawnee warriors were brought to the forefront, all carrying bow, arrows and stone axes.

The young Shawnee were going to teach a lesson. As the painted man hung there a warrior shot an arrow that lodged just below the right knee. Cheers went up as the frenzy began.

Next another young Shawnee ran at him screaming like he was going to end it all with his ax. He stopped short and chopped his left foot across the instep.

Another arrow was shot and it landed in the left leg just below the knee.

Colonel Charles Dahnmon Whitt

Dahnmon's Fantastic Dream

The other warrior was made to watch every detail. I am sure he wondered if he would be next.

Now another Shawnee ran with his ax just like the first, but he hit the ankle so hard the foot fell to the ground. Blood was running out profusely. The torch was applied and the burning cauterized the wound stopping the flow.

The young warriors were in frenzy and they made some of the most un-godliest sounds I have ever heard.

They took their time, both feet were gone then both legs. It was an awful thing to witness, but I had to put up a front of bravery. The whole tribe was gathered as if watching something beautiful.

Another young Shawnee ran up and gave the victim a lick in the groan with an upward swing from his stone war club. The victim gave out a scream at this which brought many cheers from the town.

Lord God almighty, how long will this go on, I thought to myself.

This went on for hours as the intruder was systematically being dismembered.

He hung there with black stubs that was once strong legs.

Colonel Charles Dahnmon Whitt

Dahnmon's Fantastic Dream

He could look down on his tormentors and also see his friend being made to watch every gruesome detail.

A young Shawnee walked forward with a spear and stuck it into his right eye just enough to blind him in that eye.

Oh! I wish they would just finish him off and end the pain. I think the painted warrior with no legs was already in shock and not feeling the pain.

A Shawnee shot an arrow into his right arm, another stepped up and fired a shot at the left arm and it was a glancing blow and the arrow found its mark in the chest of a little girl.

The crowd went wild and the little girl died quickly. They picked her up and carried her above their heads all around the town. I thought they would be mad at the young warrior that shot the arrow, but no, they were enraged at the hanging victim instead.

A Shawnee ran to the victim and severed his right hand from the arm. He hung there in a crooked state with his head on his left shoulder. The neck was exposed so another warrior ran up and with a vicious blow dropped the head to the ground. It was an awful sound.

Colonel Charles Dahnmon Whitt

Dahnmon's Fantastic Dream

The warrior took a long pole and stuck it up through the neck and the head was mounted about ten feet above the ground. The one good eye seemed to be scornfully watching his adversaries.

There was hanging one arm and hand on one thong, and the torso and arm on the other thong. I am sure the heart had stopped by now and he was dead but it went on further. The thongs were cut and the remaining parts were chopped by the Shawnee men. Next came a crowd of squaws welding war clubs and they beat what remained into the bloody ground. It was all I could do not to vomit.

There was nothing but a bloody mud hole.

The other warrior that had been brought and made to watch was pulled to his feet. Chief Panther addressed him harshly and shoved him toward the south. Thank God, they were letting this young man go back to tell the gory details and warn the southern Indians to stay away from Shawnee hunting grounds. The young man looked at the chief over his shoulder and walked proudly toward the south side of the town. As he got to the edge he went into a jog and never looked back.

I have never seen anything like this in either of my lives. I have read of torture, but to witness it as I did there is no comparison.

Colonel Charles Dahnmon Whitt

Dahnmon's Fantastic Dream

I had at least for now lost respect for these blood thirsty savages.

Lord, I wish I was back home; I know if I make a mistake I could end up just like this young man that marked the spot of his death only with a blood spot in the dirt.

Colonel Charles Dahnmon Whitt

Dahnmon's Fantastic Dream
A Trip With Co-o-nah

The next day everything was back to normal on Town Hill. It was just as if nothing had happened with the capture of the two intruders from the southern tribe.

One was free and I think hastily traveling south. The other was only a bloody spot in the dirt. I will never forget this ordeal, whether it is a dream or for real.

The Panther sent out regular scouting parties to insure that there were no more trespassers into Shawnee hunting grounds.

Co-o-nah wanted to take a trip, I think to show me about and to bond more deeply with me. He came to me and let me know about his plan. It would be just the two of us.

We took our bows and pouches of food. We also wore outer garments and leggings to protect us from the wilderness and the cool mountain air.

I noticed that my Indian friends didn't pay much attention to time. If they wanted to do something, they did it.

Colonel Charles Dahnmon Whitt

Dahnmon's Fantastic Dream

We went down from Town Hill and stopped at the creek, ("Lick Lock," or "Lick Lot"), and took a long refreshing drink. We were headed toward the Paint Lick hunting grounds. We were in the deep woods soon and following the warrior's path. Co-o-nah took the lead but we walked side by side in the wider parts of the path.

It got dark in the east woodland very quickly, so Co-o-nah had me gather a bunch of firewood while he sparked a fire with his flint. The fire would serve two purposes, warmth and protection from the big predators that roamed this woodland.

We had settled for the night under a nice rock-house. Co-o-nah had taken a limb and raked the leaves about to uncover any snakes or spiders that might want to sleep with us.

With nothing hiding in the leaves, Co-o-nah took the limb and fashioned us beds up under the rock.

With the fire burning we had eaten from our pouch. We sat there looking at the fire not saying much and Co-o-nah pulled out his pipe and filled it with kinnikinnick. (Various herbs and tobacco, sometimes it contained some marijuana.)

Co-o-nah lit the pipe with a twig from the campfire by taking long easy puffs. After he had it burning, he passed it over to me.

Colonel Charles Dahnmon Whitt

Dahnmon's Fantastic Dream

I noticed Co-o-nah as he was puffing the pipe that his Indian features really stood out with the high cheek bones and chiseled face.

I puffed on the pipe a few times and felt myself relax. It had a nice aroma and a satisfying flavor. I think something was in it that caused me to relax also.

We passed the pipe back and forth enjoying the time and smoke. I don't know what was in it, but it doesn't matter anyway, I am just having a dream I thought. Right?

We sat there in the deep woodland of 1600's Clinch Valley and enjoyed the company.

Co-o-nah took out his sharp stone knife from its sheath and opened up his right hand with his palm up.

I was wondering what he was going to do next when he looked at me and showed me his open palm. Next he gently pulled the razor sharp flint across his palm just enough to draw blood.

Next Co-o-nah handed me the knife, handle first. I opened my right palm and did likewise. I could barely feel the blade cut into the skin. I looked and noticed I had brought the blood.

Colonel Charles Dahnmon Whitt

Dahnmon's Fantastic Dream

Co-o-nah had a solemn look on his face as he put his right palm on mine and gently squeezed. I pushed my palm against his to allow our blood to mix. We were becoming bonded even more with the gripping of the right hands in a good shake. We were now brothers bonded by blood. I wondered if the right hand was significant or if he was left handed. I think he was left-handed.

We settled back into our beds and I fell asleep quickly. In the middle of the dark night I was awaken slightly. I cracked open my eyes and saw Co-o-nah putting more wood on the fire. Next I heard the scream of a panther and knew this must be what had awakened us. Co-o-nah motioned for me to go back to sleep as all was well.

In the morning when we were ready to travel we put out the fire by peeing on it. I felt funny doing this but you might say we killed two birds with one stone.

Co-o-nah took a piece of brush and raked the area down to make it look more natural and hide the fact that someone had been there.

We traveled to the familiar paint lick that the Shawnees loved so dearly. I thought maybe we had come to hunt, but Co-o-nah led me on a trail that skirted the lick with great herds of animals.

Colonel Charles Dahnmon Whitt

Dahnmon's Fantastic Dream

He took me up the mountain by the winding trail that had been engineered by the many animals that come here.

We were about halfway up Paint Lick Mountain when we heard a growl not far off the trail. We froze and Co-o-nah's sharp eyes spotted a big black bear standing but mostly hidden by a tree.

He smiled at me as if to say, "Look at the bear, he is being our friend."

I wasn't so sure he was being friendly; he was mighty big and strong.

We went ahead up the trail and we did not brother Mister Bear, nor did he brother us. I kept looking back over my shoulder to see if the bear might be following us. The bear stayed where he was and I reckon he figured we all share God's woodland.

I didn't know where my blood-brother Co-o-nah was taking me, but I had an idea he wanted to share something with me.

Colonel Charles Dahnmon Whitt

Dahnmon's Fantastic Dream

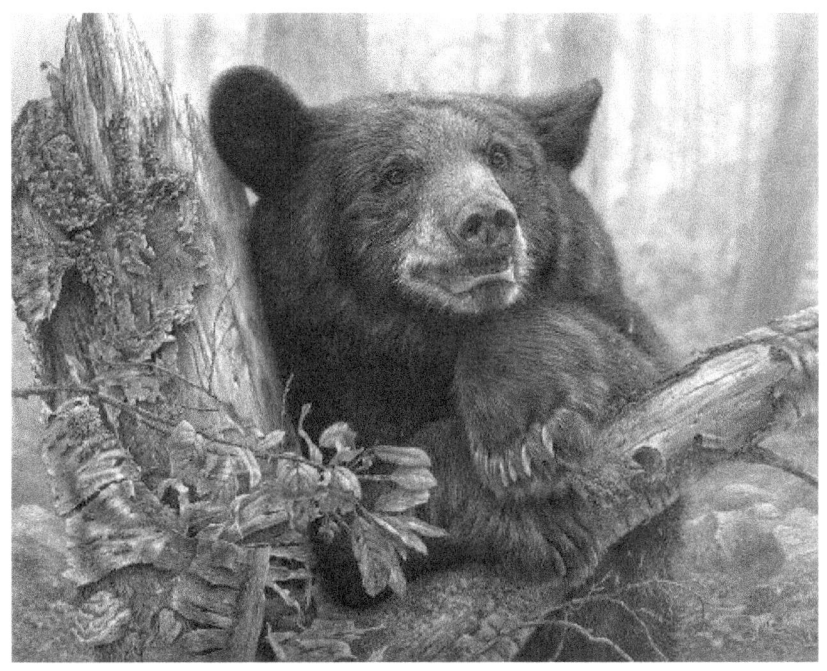

My Mister Bear

Colonel Charles Dahnmon Whitt

Dahnmon's Fantastic Dream
Painted Mountain

Finally in the afternoon Co-o-nah guided me to a special place where the cliffs stood out of the ground like a wall. There it was:

The rock wall had numerous paintings on them. I did not know the meaning of all of these paintings, but I suspect they are a form of writing and I bet they have to do with the great hunting grounds at the salt lick below.

Co-o-nah signed that the paintings on the cliff were there to protect and mark the location of the hunting grounds below at the Salt Lick. He held his hand on his forehead as if blocking the sun and looked straight down the mountain where the lick was located.

Back in the 21st century I had heard about these paintings here on Paint Lick Mountain, but I never got to see them.

I was really pleased that Co-o-nah honored me by showing this Indian treasure to me.

Colonel Charles Dahnmon Whitt

Dahnmon's Fantastic Dream

To my surprise he took a few minutes to mix up something in the dirt and made paint the color of the paintings. He went to the paintings and was very careful to touch up any that had faded or damaged. What a thrill to be here and witness this.

After he was satisfied with his work on the cliff he smiled and signed for me to gather fire wood as he did the evening before.

It looks like we are going to spend the night here in this sacred place. I see how this place is so important to the Indians and how this mountain got its name; "Painted Mountain," to the Indians or "Paint Lick Mountain" to those in the 21st century.

We had a fire and food as the night closed in on us on top of the mountain. We sat there in the dusk and looked down into the darkening valley below.

I think back to the 21st century and remember that my dad had actually lived in the valley, but it sure didn't look like it does in 1600. This was a wonderful day for me. We smoked the pipe and relaxed into sleep.

Colonel Charles Dahnmon Whitt

Dahnmon's Fantastic Dream

The Paint Lick Mountain Pictograph Archaeological Site in Tazewell County consists of a group of twenty pictographs on a rock cliff. First investigated by archaeologists late in the nineteenth century, the geometric-, animal-, and human-form designs likely were made by Virginia Indians of unknown identity and at an unknown time. There are only two known examples of such pictographs in Virginia—the other is at Little Mountain in Nottoway County—and such representations were not recorded by the early settlers of the Virginia colony. The soft mudstone at Paint Lick Mountain, rich in iron oxide, provided the red pigment used to create the pictographs, which collectively likely reflect spiritual and cognitive aspects of Indian culture. As a tangible expression of a prehistoric social connection to the landscape of Southwest Virginia, the site retains a

Colonel Charles Dahnmon Whitt

Dahnmon's Fantastic Dream

deep significance for Indian communities in Virginia and surrounding states.

Site Description

There are twenty documented pictographs at Paint Lick Mountain, ranging from geometric designs to human and animal forms. Some pictographs even combine human and animal characteristics or human characteristics and geometric shapes. While the pictographs of a running deer and the profile view of a roosting bird were executed with a degree of realism, most of the pictographs are more abstract. Of note, the pictographs include a series of bird images ranging from single birds in flight to a bird with two heads and a faded figure that appears to represent two birds joined together. More abstract is a pictograph composed of concentric circles with two L-shaped appendages that resemble human legs and feet. Some of the pictographs remain vivid while others have faded, and a few areas of the quartzite cliff contain discolorations that may be natural or evidence of additional faded images.

Colonel Charles Dahnmon Whitt

Dahnmon's Fantastic Dream

The Investigations

An 1871 geologic report for Southwest Virginia contained the first published reference to the "Indian Paintings" on Paint Lick Mountain, although the pictographs likely were part of local knowledge much earlier. In 1888, a Smithsonian Institution ethnologist wrote the first detailed account of the images, incorporating it into a lengthy monograph on "Indian Picture Writing" in North America. In 1969, in response to a report filed by Virginia Department of Historic Resources archaeologist Howard A. McCord, the Paint Lick Mountain pictographs were listed on the Virginia Landmarks Register and the National Register of Historic Places. And in the years that followed, archaeologists continued to assess the condition of the site, photographing it for the first time in 1975 and making comparative photographic studies in 1980 and 2009. In the meantime, the property owners, who restrict access to the site, led field trips that allowed the public to view the pictographs.

Colonel Charles Dahnmon Whitt

Dahnmon's Fantastic Dream
My Gobbler

Next morning we heard the flapping of wings as the big turkeys came down from their roosts. Next we heard the gobble, gobble of the birds talking to each other.

Co-o-nah signed for me to make ready my bow and follow him. We were hiding behind a bolder and there was some brush on the side in which I slipped into. Co-o-nah put both hands to his mouth and began to talk turkey to the birds. Gobble; gobble, from behind the bolder brought abrupt attention to the big Tom Turkey.

Co-o-nah sounded just like a turkey and ol' Tom trotted toward me. I was in a frozen position but had my bow fully drawn. The gobble, gobble, sounded from behind me again and Tom came within a few yards of me and I let go with the flint tipped missile. I nailed that ol' bird and he flopped about and raised quite a fuss. I held my position as the other birds scattered in the opposite direction. I

Colonel Charles Dahnmon Whitt

Dahnmon's Fantastic Dream

looked over my shoulder to see a big smile on my blood-brothers face.

Well we had turkey for breakfast and feathers for our hair.

We were in no hurry to get back to Town Hill. (Richlands) We traveled about the area and Co-o-nah escorted me all around the area that is now Tazewell County. In all of both of my lives, I have never seen such beauty. We went to a place where a river came right out of the ground; I recognized it as "Maiden's Spring." It sure looked different with the great woodland canopy over everything. I knew this river to be, "Little River," a fork of the Clinch.

Next we traveled to the flat hill that the town of Tazewell now sits on. We went up and down the area they now call "Baptist Valley." We swam in the rivers and fished for our suppers. I had pretty much forgotten the savage side of the Indians by now. I found that those in a tribe are loved and protected, while any enemy better beware. Indians do not lie to each other, but all is fair in war against an enemy.

Colonel Charles Dahnmon Whitt

Dahnmon's Fantastic Dream

Co-o-nah and I were out in a wild land and it seemed that we were the only people in the world. He was special to me now that we are blood-brothers, yet I know I would never want to cross him.

I hated to go back to Town Hill because of the horror I saw there. When we were coming into the Indian town we were greeted by almost the whole village. I have never seen such love. I saw no sign that the intruding braves from the south had ever been there.

Life was good again as I seemed to fit in better each day. Co-o-nah informed all my red friends that he and I were now brothers and this made everyone happy. I now was a full-fledged Shawnee as far as they were concerned.

At night I would lay awake and think about my dear wife and grown children. I wonder how they were handling my being gone.

Will I die here with my Indian friends and will that be what sends me back to the future. Could this be

Colonel Charles Dahnmon Whitt

Dahnmon's Fantastic Dream

the only future I have? I also think about waking up in the 21st century with this fantastic tale to tell. Who in this world would believe me? Also I wonder what the Indians in 1600 thought about their visitor from the future.

Colonel Charles Dahnmon Whitt

Dahnmon's Fantastic Dream
Back to the Future

One day I was down on the Clinch fishing with my red friends. We were roughly a quarter of a mile from Town Hill when the sky turned to night as the wind blew like I have never seen before in either of my lives.

My friends and I decided we better get back to our lodges as quick as possible. So we made a run for it. At my age I could not run as fast as the other men. By now we were dodging big limbs as the wind tore at the great trees. Dust and dirt were getting in my eyes, I could hardly see. Big branches were hitting all about.

I never saw it coming, but I was struck in the head by a big falling limb. I was out like a light.

I was there in the dark for a while and then I saw this bright light. I instinctively headed toward the light.

I heard a voice that sounded like it was far away, "Mister Whitt," are you awake?

The voice got closer and I opened my eyes to see a nurse all in white talking to me. I first thought she was an angel.

Colonel Charles Dahnmon Whitt

Dahnmon's Fantastic Dream

"Where am I?" I asked?

"Mister Whitt you are in the ICU here at the hospital, you have been asleep for a couple of weeks," said the nurse.

"What happened to me?" I asked?

"You had a really bad experience with your sleeping pills, an allergic reaction," she said.

"Which hospital am I in?" I asked?

"The Clinch Valley Clinic right here on Town Hill," she answered.

"I have been back with the Indians," I said in a serious tone.

She smiled at me and said, "You have been somewhere for sure."

I could see that this true tale would never be believed.

I looked at my palm and sure enough there was the scar from my cutting it to become blood-brothers with Co-o-nah.

I told the nurse about how I got the scar.

Colonel Charles Dahnmon Whitt

Dahnmon's Fantastic Dream

She looked at it and smiled, "you did get cut there some time ago," she said.

I knew exactly where it came from. No one will ever convince me that I did not go back to the Indians.

I thought of the paintings on Paint Lick Mountain and know exactly what they look like because I saw them in 1600.

My wife and family were called and they all came to the hospital. I was sitting up and eating that nasty hospital food and complaining about being here. I was ready to go back home to Kentucky.

I was so glad to see my wife (Sharon) and family, and I would be telling this wonderful tale to the day I die. I wonder how my brother, Co-o-nah is and what he thought after I was gone.

The End

Colonel Charles Dahnmon Whitt

Dahnmon's Fantastic Dream

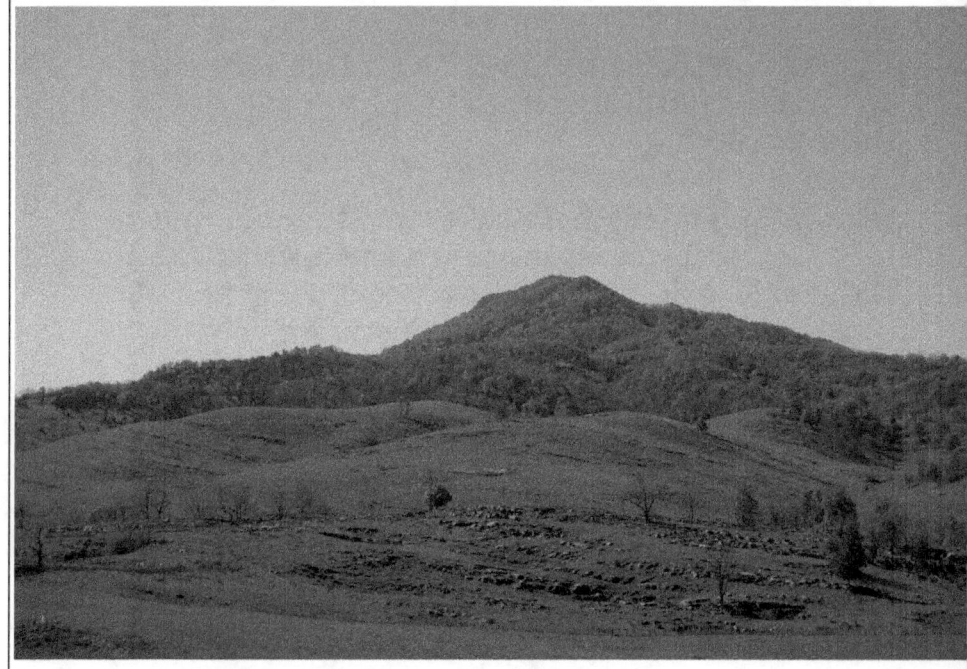

Paint Lick Mountain in 2012
Only The Indians Know

Colonel Charles Dahnmon Whitt

Dahnmon's Fantastic Dream

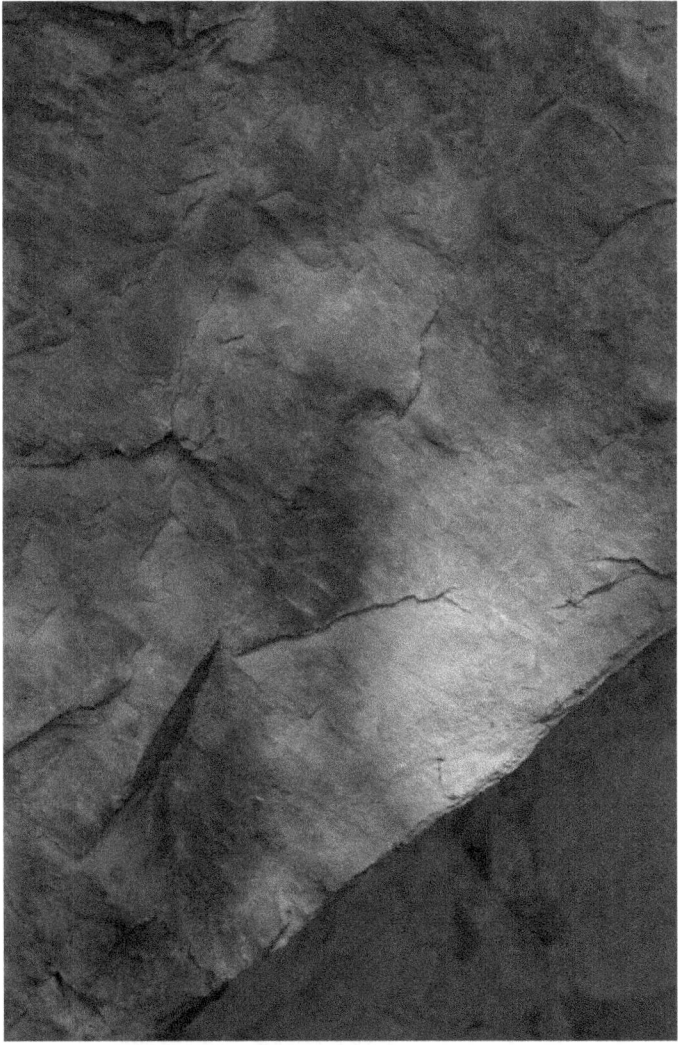

Hard to see in Black and White
It appears to be a Bird.

Colonel Charles Dahnmon Whitt

Dahnmon's Fantastic Dream

Bird under the Sun

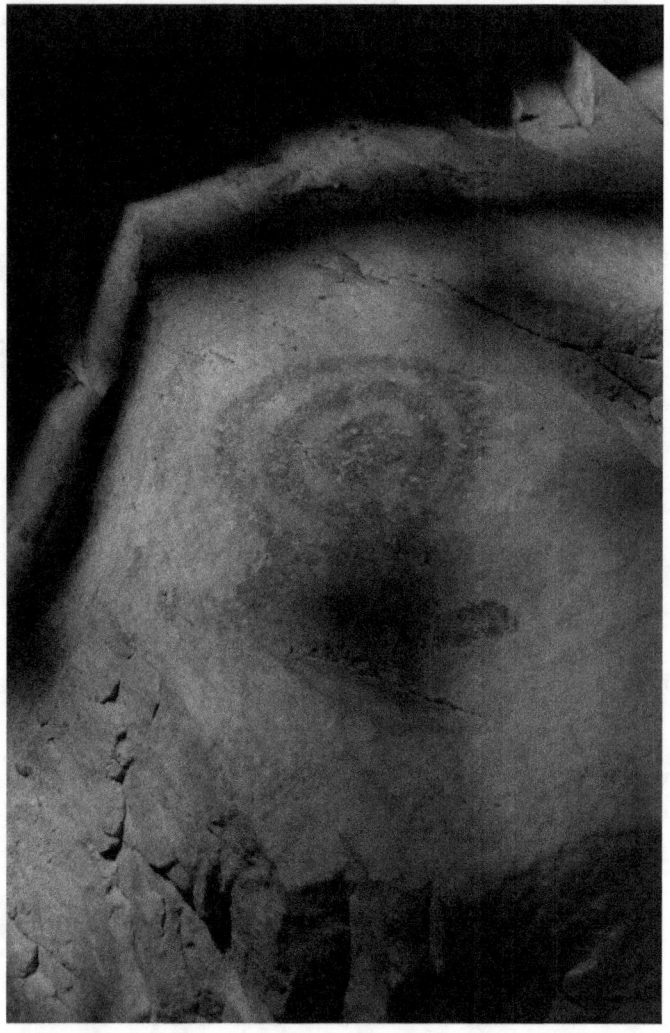

Colonel Charles Dahnmon Whitt

Dahnmon's Fantastic Dream

Town Hill today

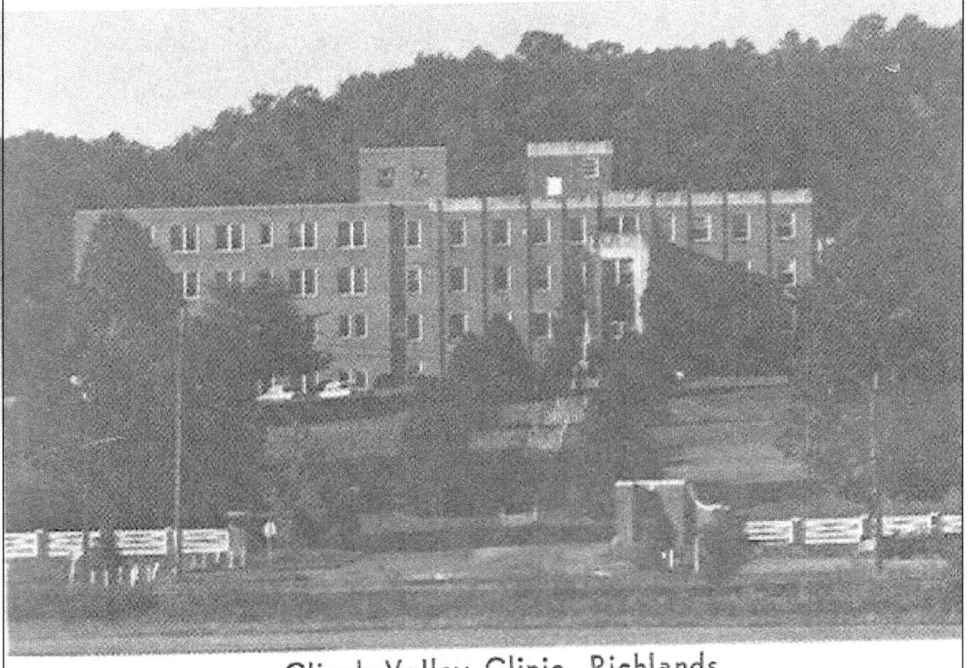

Clinch Valley Clinic, Richlands

Colonel Charles Dahnmon Whitt

Dahnmon's Fantastic Dream

Extra:

Dahnmon's Poems

1.

Winter is getting weak,

If I get through March,

I will live another year.

I have seen the robins and buzzards.

I have seen the groundhogs peeping out.

Yes spring is coming, God is fully alive.

The Earth is wakening,

An example of the great resurrection!

I am alive and I am glad!

Colonel Charles Dahnmon Whitt

Dahnmon's Fantastic Dream

2.

The days are getting longer,

The sun shines bright.

Now we prepare to come out of winter's night.

What is my purpose?

What am I to do?

I think spring is just about here.

It is time to get my fishing pole as the hungry fish look for my worms!

Yes the Sun shines bright and I am glad!

Colonel Charles Dahnmon Whitt

Dahnmon's Fantastic Dream

3.

The farmer turns the winter ground.

The robins follow to pick up the worms!

The creeks are clear.

The animals are losing their winter fur!

What does this mean? What does it say?

Jesus the master is showing His way!

The earth is awake,

Jesus shows us that He is alive.

Colonel Charles Dahnmon Whitt

Dahnmon's Fantastic Dream

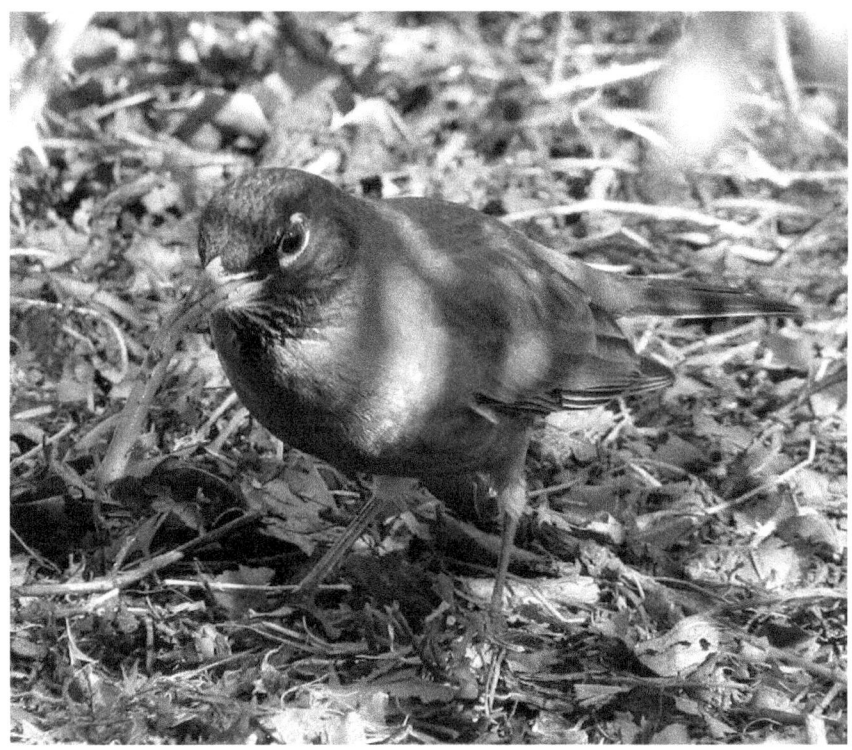

Spring's Robin

Colonel Charles Dahnmon Whitt

Dahnmon's Fantastic Dream

4.

It is the time of LENT!

Have we received the message to repent?

Jesus is coming in forty days.

We celebrate this, the Easter Way!

Jesus died for you and me.

They hung Him on a rugged tree.

Can we not repent?

God's love was Heaven sent!

Colonel Charles Dahnmon Whitt

Dahnmon's Fantastic Dream

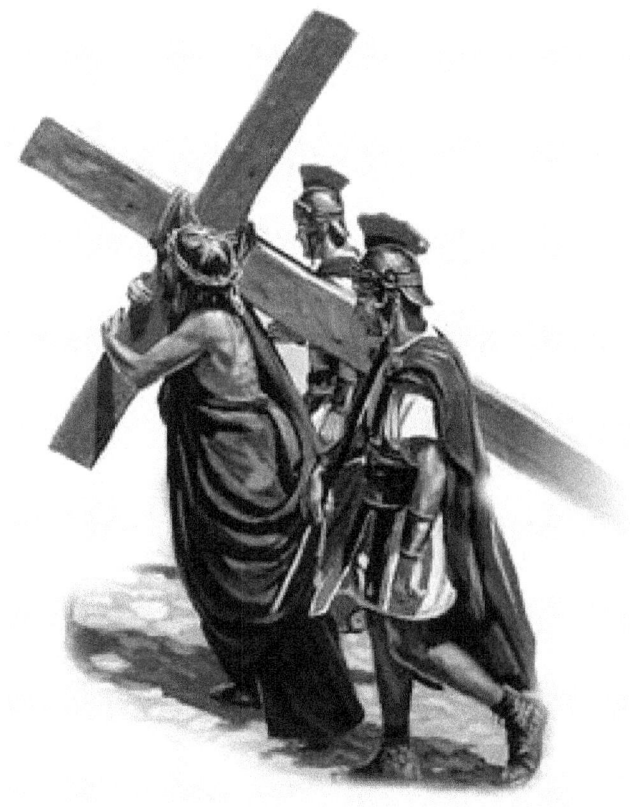

Colonel Charles Dahnmon Whitt

Dahnmon's Fantastic Dream

5.

Have you talked to God today?

Too busy, you say!

Do you race your way to work?

Did you greet your friends today?

Don't you even have time to say, Hey?

What if God took his eyes off you?

What if God was too busy for you?

Race through life you fool!

Colonel Charles Dahnmon Whitt

Dahnmon's Fantastic Dream

6.

Can you remember what they said?

Do unto others,

As you would have them do unto you.

I remember that,

It's the Golden Rule.

It will always work,

Unless you are a total jerk.

Love your neighbor; it will give you better luck!

Colonel Charles Dahnmon Whitt

Dahnmon's Fantastic Dream

7.

Seasons come and seasons go,

Lord, hurry and get us out of the snow!

I love the spring and the scattered showers.

I just can't wait to see the flowers.

Read your Bible about Jesus waking up.

The spring season reminds us so much.

How on that Easter day, Jesus woke up.

God the Father touched His Son to rise again.

Colonel Charles Dahnmon Whitt

Dahnmon's Fantastic Dream

8.

Have you ever been on a slippery rock creek?

Were you seeking to catch a fish from the deep?

The water was so cool and the air smelled so fair.

I did not expect to see any danger there.

From upstream came a roar.

I could hardly believe my eyes.

A giant wave comes my way.

God told me boldly, get out of its way.

Colonel Charles Dahnmon Whitt

Dahnmon's Fantastic Dream

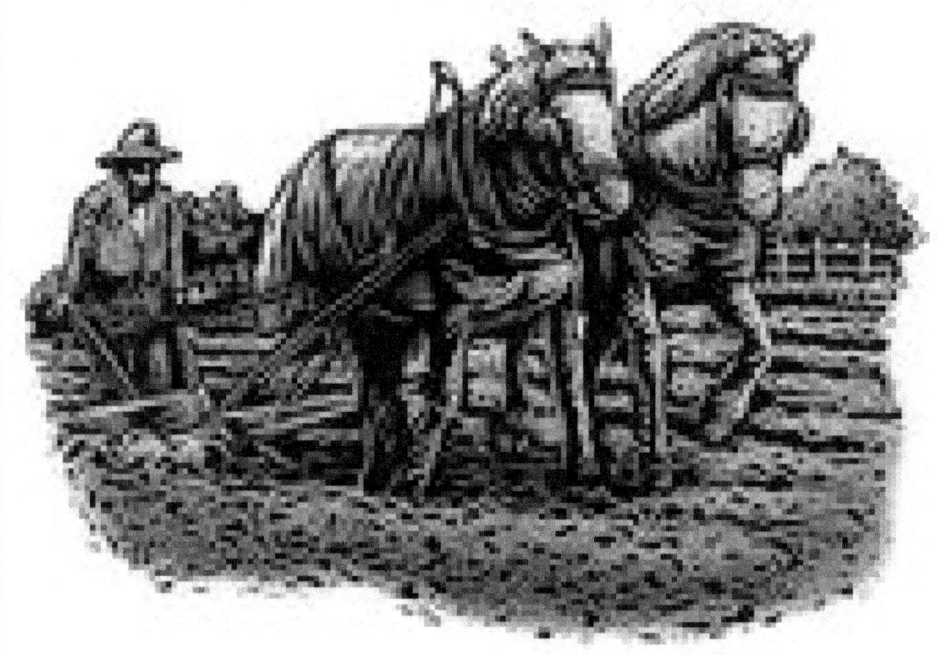

The Farmer of old.

Colonel Charles Dahnmon Whitt

Dahnmon's Fantastic Dream

9.

The days of horses are past.

Man thinks new automobiles will last.

Have we gone forward or back?

You say you would rather ride a Cadillac!

Which is better, God's green earth, or a smoky sky?

Which one will make you die?

Horses give back to the earth.

Will we die of gasoline smoke? Choke!

Colonel Charles Dahnmon Whitt

Dahnmon's Fantastic Dream

10.

Oh! What a waste,

So many presume to have fun.

These folks never see the sun.

They search for something, they know not what.

Could it be God?

Drugs and strong drink has taken His place.

Poor people, so dumb and numb.

If they would just try God!

Colonel Charles Dahnmon Whitt

Dahnmon's Fantastic Dream

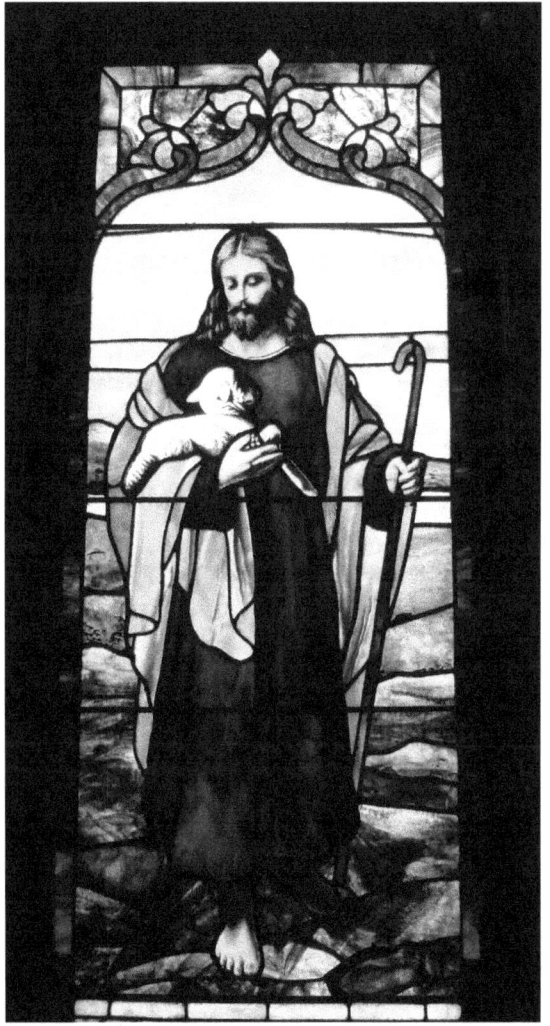

Window in Mead Memorial United Methodist Church
Russell, Kentucky

The Good Shepherd
Colonel Charles Dahnmon Whitt

Dahnmon's Fantastic Dream

11.

The Old White Church of Raven,

What a dandy it was.

It was a witness to Christ for many years.

It was plain and simple, it was hot and it was cold.

It was weather beaten but stood to gain the soul.

It had two doors in front, one for the ladies and one for the gents.

Many ol preachers preached the word of God.

The Holy Spirit was always there.

Colonel Charles Dahnmon Whitt

Dahnmon's Fantastic Dream

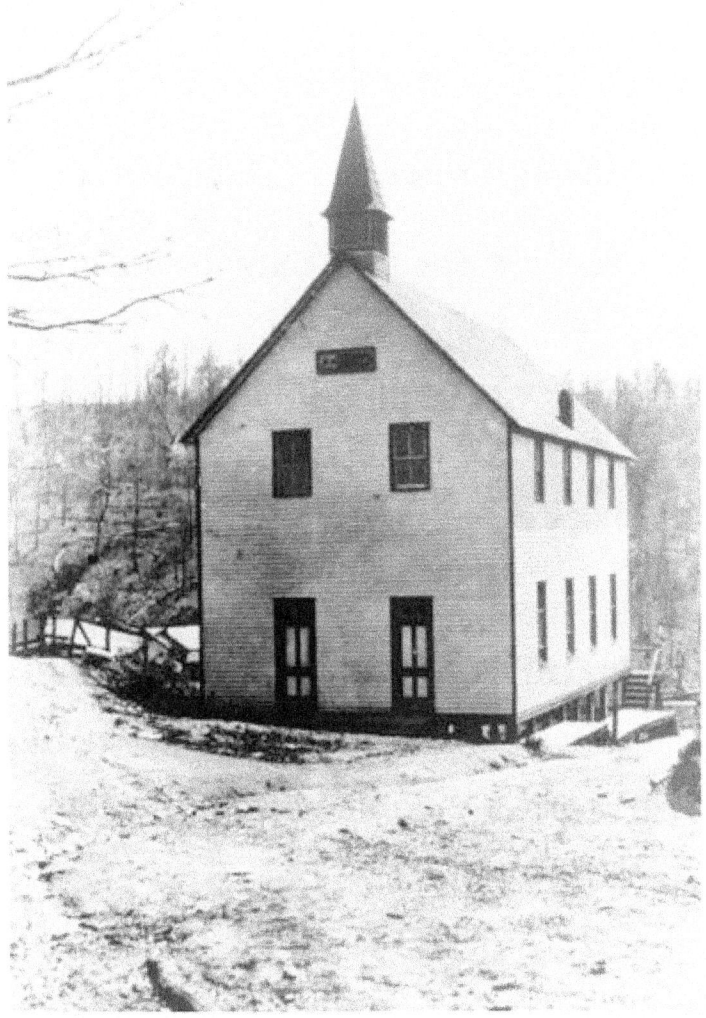

The Old White Church, Raven, VA
Picture taken in 1910

Colonel Charles Dahnmon Whitt

Dahnmon's Fantastic Dream

12.

How Did I Get Here?

How did I get here, let me see!

I started out as a baby on my mama's knee!

I ate like a pig and grew real keen!

I went to school, looked around and said; how did I get here?

Shut up, sit down, learn that spelling and math; Oh my goodness, my head is full and a spinning!

I looked around again; how did I get here?

I went to high school, but didn't quite fit in!

I took my classes but did not do well! How did I get here?

Colonel Charles Dahnmon Whitt

Dahnmon's Fantastic Dream

I took up football, but I was too small
and slow as a snail; coach said keep my
head up, but all I got was a blooded nose.
How did I get here?

I met a Navy Man, he told me he had
a plan for me; I took the test that all
thought I would flunk! I aced that sucker
and was promised the world, or was it to
see the world?

They flew me to boot camp, I felt just
fine! Next thing I knew I was cussed down
to the ground! How did I get here?

I did real well; they said I was swell,
could I sign up for another tour?

"No" I said, "you got me once!" I ran
and checked out and got out of that
place!

I was so pleased; how did I get here?

Colonel Charles Dahnmon Whitt

Dahnmon's Fantastic Dream

I met a woman; I thought she was
sweet as honey! She departed for another!
How did I get here?

I worked for the man, never had a plan,
how will I get out of here?

Will I ever retire; I doubt I will ever make
it! How did I get here?

I met another woman, this one is for
me! How did I get here?

I met my Lord Jesus and He really
had a plan! How did I get here?

Finally I died and went to this beautiful
place! No crying, no pain, just walking
around Heaven all day!

How did I get here? I know now, It was
the Lord Jesus who saved me!
John 3:16

13.

Colonel Charles Dahnmon Whitt

Dahnmon's Fantastic Dream

A New Year!

We all get to start over as a new year
comes to town!

Some face it with a smile; some face it
with a frown.

Up north is very cold, but down south it is
pleasant and warm!

Some treat it with love, some look on it
as harm!

We all know the past, and some of it was
not fun!

We are in the present, which often gives
us alarm!

We look to the future with glee!

We all hope it has the key!

Colonel Charles Dahnmon Whitt

Dahnmon's Fantastic Dream

No matter how old we get, we remember the past as if happened yesterday!

We don't know what to do in the present day!

Now we can start over and hope for a new day!

What is our hope? What is our prayer?

Should we talk about it, or will we jinx whatever is there?

Our life is like the leaves on a tree!

We start out little and green!

We grow up and experience the warm summer breeze!

As our life rolls on we run out of time, we look to the past, and remember the great times!

Colonel Charles Dahnmon Whitt

Dahnmon's Fantastic Dream

As we get older we tire and wrinkle up!

Looks like the future is gone, we may as well give up!

But let's not give up as we fall to the ground, our lives will give hope to the new little green ones!

God calls us to live and to help the ones on the ground!

God is our hope and leads us along!

So this New Year's Day, lets contemplate, stop and pray!

The Good Lord has given us another day!

Colonel Charles Dahnmon Whitt

Dahnmon's Fantastic Dream

14.

What Price?

What "Price" will you give? Don't worry it's free!

Is there really a Heaven? Is there really a Hell?

God wrote the word, it is for us to read!

If God wrote the word, it is for us to read!

If God wrote the word, it is for us to heed!

Yes there is a Heaven, the price has been paid!

Yes there is a Hell! For those that don't heed, their fate is made!

Colonel Charles Dahnmon Whitt

Dahnmon's Fantastic Dream

**So remember with Jesus the price
has been paid!**

So remember with Satan our fate is made!

Colonel Charles Dahnmon Whitt

Dahnmon's Fantastic Dream

15.

What Is A Creek?

What is a creek, it is Heaven sent!

It is a joy to see and refreshing for a boy to play in!

A creek is like a river but God made it small!

It was just right for a boy like me!

My Mommy said stay away from there, you will get hurt, but it drew me like a magnet!

The creek had minnows, those delightful little fish! It had crawdads that looked like little lobsters!

It had big tree roots that stuck out into the water; watch out here for the scary wiggling snake!

Colonel Charles Dahnmon Whitt

Dahnmon's Fantastic Dream

It had tall weeds that grew along its banks, Oh! What a delightful place!

I learned so much about life while just playing along the creek!

It had ducks, and under its banks it had muskrats too!

I caught my first fish, even though it was small, It meant so much to a boy like me!

It did have some traps I soon learned about; the three leafed Poison Ivy was waiting for me!

When I think of my life and all that I have been through, it was that little creek that prepared me so well!

It had training, and comfort too!

I fell through its ice and was really

Colonel Charles Dahnmon Whitt

Dahnmon's Fantastic Dream

cold! I found that the world was much like this too, if you skate on thin ice you will fall in!

It was refreshing in summer to splash and play, I have never found anything better in this world!

God made my creek, it was just right for a boy like me!

Colonel Charles Dahnmon Whitt

Dahnmon's Fantastic Dream

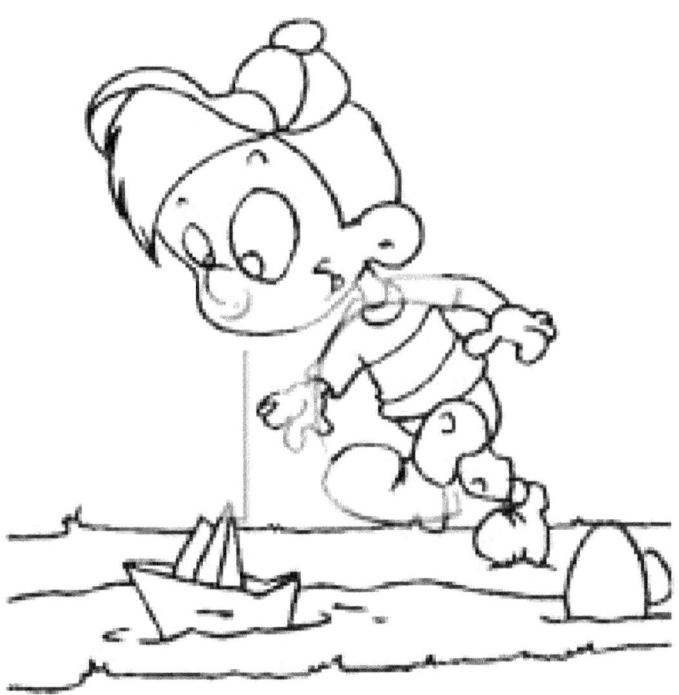

Boy and His Creek

Colonel Charles Dahnmon Whitt

Dahnmon's Fantastic Dream

16.

Death struck at Cold Harbor June 3, 1864

Gettysburg was over, Grant pushed to win.

Lee's Army was lined with the river to their backs,

There were no slackers, just brave determined boys in gray.

Grant was so sure of a win he sent thousands to their doom.

Lee's men were behind a zigzag breast-work and had plenty of lead.

The Bloody 29th was in center and ready to defend.

Grant's men wrote their wills and pinned them inside their coats.

Colonel Charles Dahnmon Whitt

Dahnmon's Fantastic Dream

General Lee must stop Grant here today.

Grant marched his men into the guns of hell.

The Confederates turned lose on the boys in blue; seven thousand fell in ten minutes.

The boys of gray felt some shame as they looked on with their scorched faces.

General Grant knew he would not get through.

He never called a truce to gather the dead, but instead he shook his head.

General Grant left his dead and started to try another route to Richmond town.

The boys in gray hung in their trenches.

Three hot days the bodies begin to swell.

Colonel Charles Dahnmon Whitt

Dahnmon's Fantastic Dream

It was an awful sight, as the hogs came out to dine.

General Lee found out what Grant was up to,

So he trotted the boys in gray to get between Grant and Richmond Town.

Shame was felt on both sides of the fence,

Both sides were ashamed of Grant's disgrace;

The young boys in blue fell like leaves on a fall day.

Colonel Charles Dahnmon Whitt

Dahnmon's Fantastic Dream

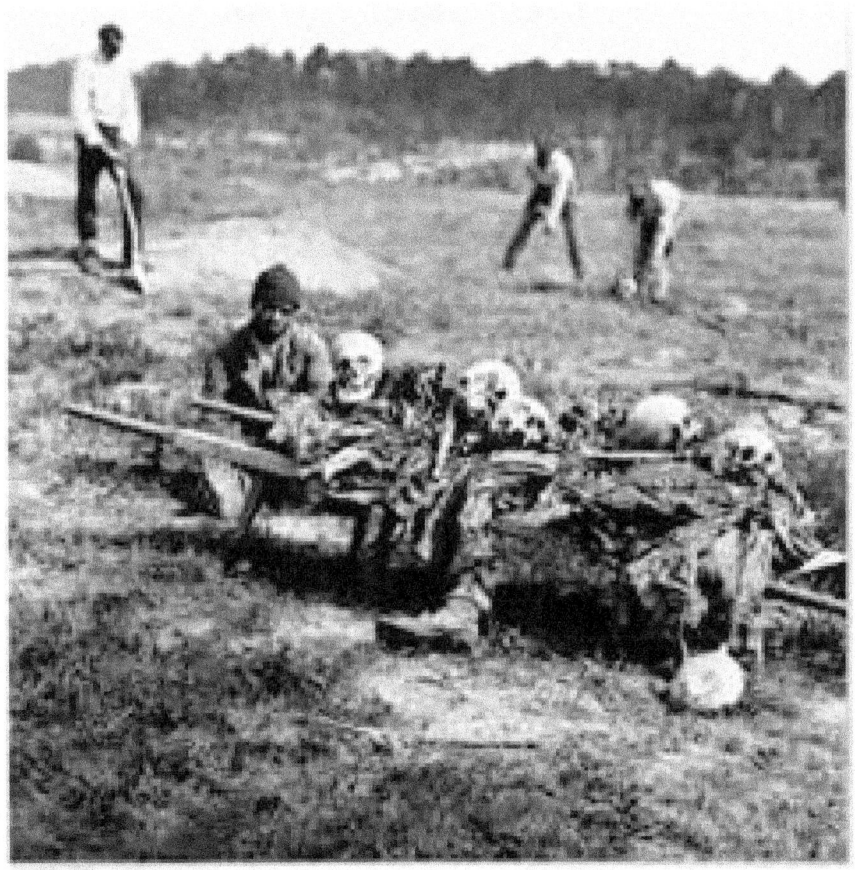

Picking up bones in 1865, at Cold Harbor.

Colonel Charles Dahnmon Whitt

Dahnmon's Fantastic Dream

17.

The Great Silver Towers

I went to New York as a Sheet Metal Man.

I only went for a job, this turned out to be a great plan.

I had never seen such a job, it was growing tall.

There were two that grew out of the ground.

The roots were so deep, they were seven stories down.

She reached into the sky one hundred ten stories high.

The hippies came out to protest but didn't stay long,

Big bolts and nuts came crashing down.

Colonel Charles Dahnmon Whitt

Dahnmon's Fantastic Dream

**Now I wonder who would accidentally drop
these bombs from so high.**

We got them built and America was proud,

**The damn dumb, Muslins knocked them
down.**

**Now all of us have cried, so many of us
have died, why, why?**

**The Silver towers are gone, but some of
her metal still floats in a boat.**

**God bless America and may the enemy
find Christ.**

Colonel Charles Dahnmon Whitt

Dahnmon's Fantastic Dream

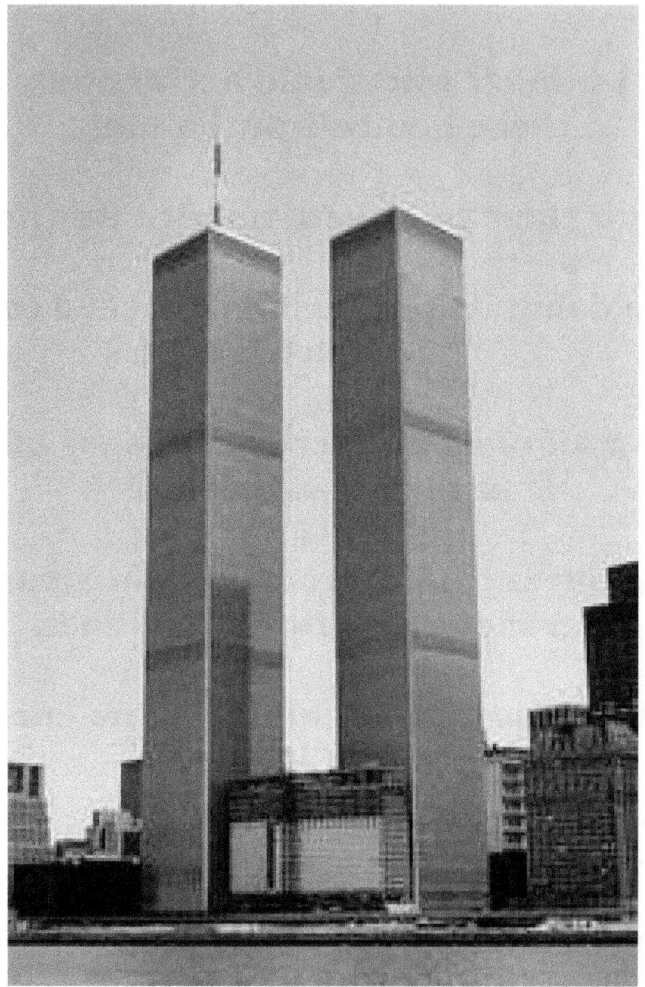

The World Trade Center as seen in the New York sky line.
September 11, 2001 they fell.

Colonel Charles Dahnmon Whitt

Dahnmon's Fantastic Dream

Colonel Charles Dahnmon Whitt

Colonel Whitt is a native of Tazewell County Virginia, but has lived in Greenup County for forty years. He loves regional history, Civil War History, and genealogy.

With this love pushing him he has become a researcher, genealogist, and a novelist. In the last decade the Colonel has dug up an enormous amount of genealogy data and now keeps a web site with over 15,900 names to search and over 400 pictures to look at. He started research around 1999 with his first computer.

The Colonel especially loves reenactments of the War Between the States. Even though many people think that the war was fought over slavery, the Colonel has determined that slavery was brought to the forefront to gain support of the Northern Citizens. The Colonel has found that only 2% of the Confederate Soldiers owned slaves and General Grant's wife owned slaves while he led the northern armies invading the South. See the Colonel's new book, "Confederate American."

With Genealogy the Colonel found his G G Grandfather's Grave in Greenup County, KY after living in the county for thirty years. This genealogy data has led to write his books. "Legacy, The Days of

Colonel Charles Dahnmon Whitt

Dahnmon's Fantastic Dream

David Crockett Whitt," which is the story of the Colonel's Great Grand Father. This 580 page book covers the years of 1836 to 1900 and is historic-fiction. The Colonel keeps the dates, names, and places correct while letting the characters live out their lives in a harder, but simpler age. The Colonel has inserted Christian witness through-out his books in prayers, and bits of scripture from the Holy Bible. He is a member of Mead Memorial United Methodist Church in Russell, KY.

One of the Colonel's latest efforts is called "The Patriot, Hezekiah Whitt," which is the Colonel's GGG Grand Father. This work deals with the years of 1760 to 1846. Indian stories abound as these hardy people build America. It is also based on a true story, but is written in the historic-fiction fashion.

The Colonel was pleased to add a few bits to the Historic Book about Greenup County, Portsmouth and Ironton, Ohio. The Colonels books will transcend you back into history as you read. You will feel like you are back in the earlier years of America.

For more Information about the Colonel you may go to his web site at http://dahnmonwhittfamily.com and see all of his 9 published books on sale there. Contact at; Box 831, Flatwoods, KY 41139 Phone 606-836-7997 c-dahnmon@roadrunner.com

Colonel Charles Dahnmon Whitt

Dahnmon's Fantastic Dream

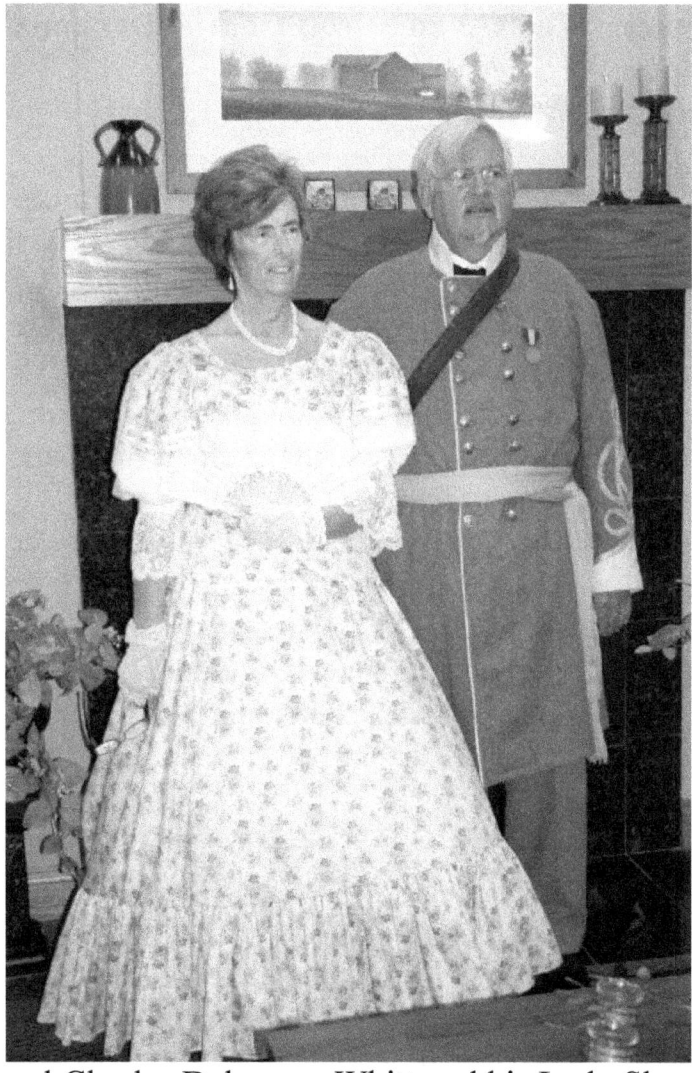

Colonel Charles Dahnmon Whitt and his Lady Sharon
Gail Cogan Whitt.

Colonel Charles Dahnmon Whitt

Dahnmon's Fantastic Dream

Biltmore Who's Who Selects Charles Dahnmon Whitt as an Executive Member of the Executive and Professional Registry

Flatwoods, KY —— Colonel Charles Dahnmom Whitt, A Kentucky Colonel, **Author** and **Publisher** of *Dahnmon Whitt Family Publishing*, has been selected as an **Honored Member of the <u>Biltmore Who's Who</u> Executive and Professional Registry**. The selection recognizes **Colonel Charles Dahnmon Whitt's** commitment to excellence in Writing and Publishing.

Colonel Whitt, a Journeyman sheet metal worker who spent over thirty-five years in the sheet metal industry before retiring in 2003, began researching genealogy in 1999. After conducting a good amount of research on Great Grandpa David Crockett Whitt, Whitt wrote a 580 page book in 2008, entitled Legacy, The Days of David Crockett Whitt.

Now overseeing his small publishing company, Dahnmon Whitt Family Publishing, **Colonel Whitt** conducts research, writes books, and promotes himself by hosting signings, festivals, reenactments and public speaking.

"My new career has taught me how to conduct research, a number of new computer skills, publishing,

Colonel Charles Dahnmon Whitt

Dahnmon's Fantastic Dream

and the art of selling books," **Colonel Whitt** said. "Having fun is always my main goal."

Inspired by God, his wife and family, **Colonel Whitt** would like to see one of his eight books see the best sellers list sometime in the future. In the meantime, he continues to write and maintain his business and that is just fine with him.

Whitt is a member of the Appalachian Ohio Valley Writer's Guild, Virginia Writer's Club, Appalachian Writers Guild, and the American Veterans Association. He is also a certified lay speaker with the United Methodist Church. **Colonel Whitt** is the author of the following books: *Legacy, The Days of David Crockett Whitt, The Patriot, Hezekiah Whitt, Dahnmon's Little Stories, Confederate American, Haunts and Spirits of the Past, Legacy 2nd Edition, The Days of David Crockett, The South Won, What If?, and Life's Journey, and now Dahnmon's Fantastic Dream.* He is the recipient of two Certificates of Recognition from the Senate of the Commonwealth of Kentucky for his research and writing abilities and recently served as Grand Marshall in a local parade.

For more information, visit http://www.dahnmonwhittfamily.com., e-mail c-dahnmon@roadrunner.com MyVideo below http://www.youtube.com/watch?v=PcuNQpN36a4&feature=youtu.be

Colonel Charles Dahnmon Whitt

www.ingramcontent.com/pod-product-compliance
Lightning Source LLC
Chambersburg PA
CBHW051542170526
45165CB00002B/848